We All Walk Together

The Loving Light Books Series

Also by Liane Rich

Loving Light

Book 17

We All Walk Together

Liane Rich

Loving Light Books
Original Copyright © 1995
Copyright © 2011 Liane

ISBN 13: 978-1-878480-17-0
ISBN 10: 1-878480-17-0

Loving Light Books:
www.lovinglightbooks.com

Also Available at:
Amazon: www.amazon.com
Barnes & Noble: www.barnesandnoble.com

Remember, you are a spiritual being and you have no roots. You are human only to house the spirit. Let the spirit float free and create for you....

The information in this series is not necessarily meant to be taken literally. It is meant to *shift* your consciousness....

Foreword

Anyone immersed in the vast body of new metaphysical knowledge is aware of the virtual symphony of voices from channeled sources throughout the world – inspirational voices that may be artistic, poetic, philosophical, religious, or scientific. And now, out of these myriad New Age voices, comes a series of books by God, channeled through Liane, revealing the frank truth in all its glory and wonder, telling us how to cleanse our bodies, gain access to our subconscious minds, clear our other selves and march back to who we are – God.

In God's books you will be introduced to a loving, powerful, gripping, exciting, and often humorous voice that reaches out and speaks ever so personally to the individual reader. As the reader's interest deepens, invariably an intimate relationship to this voice develops. It is a relationship that lasts forever, and I am quite certain I do mean forever.

Here is an accelerated program, a no-holds-barred course, where God guides us and loves us, and as needs be recommends books to us and even a movie or musical piece along the way. He (She) enters our lives and sees through our eyes, seeming to enjoy the ride as He guides us back to US, back to ALL. Here is a voice that is playful and informative, that is humorous and serious, that is gentle and powerfully divine. It is a voice that knows no barriers or restrictions, a straightforward and honest voice that caresses us when we need the warmth and pushes us when we are immobilized.

In today's New Age literature there is an avalanche of information from magnificent beings of light, information that possesses us and compels us to look at our fears and express our love. In this series of books by God, you will find truly powerful methods for making this transition from toxicity to purity, from density to light, from fear to love, and from the delusion of death to the awakening to full life. You will experience in these books the love and the power of God for it is your love to express and your power to behold. Rarely will you see more lucid steps for transformation. Read these beautiful words and rejoice in our period of awakening, our return to Home.

John Farrell, PhD., LCSW. – Psychologist, Clinical Social Worker, Senior Clinician Psychiatric Emergency Services, U.C. Davis Medical Center, Sacramento. John is also a retired Professor – California State University, Sacramento, in Health Sciences and Psychology.

We All Walk Together

Introduction

*W*hen you first began to awaken you were very excited, and you knew that your life was going to be changed. You knew you had to be in you in order to be who you are, but you never really gave it too much thought. The process of growing into yourself is quite unique and also very tedious for you at times. It's a process of rediscovering all parts of yourself, and getting acquainted with the new parts that come alive by letting go of the restrictions placed on the old parts. As you begin to move into new areas of your own beingness, you will be processing and gathering information about you to use in growing. You are learning to evolve one step at a time, and you are evolving one step at a time.

As you learn to take life a step at a time you will begin to relax. You will no longer be overwhelmed by all the what-ifs that face you as you look into your future. As you let go of greater restrictions that were placed upon you to keep you down, you will begin to feel the lightness of knowing and the lightness of awareness. As you move into knowingness and awareness you actually move away from pain and fear. Pain and fear are a part of you that is being shifted and moved. You will feel it as it goes. You will know it for how it feels and how it affects you.

You all have feelings of pain and hurt. You all fear! It is impossible at this point to not fear. You live in an environment of fear that is based on "controlling everything to keep you safe." You will move out of fear and into an environment that is based on seeing only the gifts in every situation. You will easily move when it is time and you will easily stay when it is time to stay. You will not worry about how you must not do this, or how if you do the opposite you may be making a big mistake. Everything will become clear to you and with clarity comes peace of mind.

As you learn to adjust to the renovations being done inside of you, you will begin to settle down and flow more easily. It is as though you are being adjusted and re-adjusted from the inside. You are being prepared to accept greater parts of yourself so that you might operate from more than ten percent of yourself. You are growing into all of yourself so that you might gain your full potential back. As you open up to receive more of "you," I wish you to remember to be kind and gentle with your response to being stretched so big.

You have never gotten so pulled and so stretched as you will to receive greater quantities of you. As you receive the energy that is you, your life will begin to change and you will begin to shift and grow. As you shift and grow you will have situations arise that you completely do not understand. Do not be frightened. Your growth has to do with moving into new uncharted areas and it has to do with "expansion." The expansion of you is the greatest gift you will give to yourself. It is the ability to own and accept more of the self than a tiny pinpoint. It is the ability to rise to new levels of awareness within the self, and it is the ability to ascend to new heights. The level of awareness is directly connected to the level of light that you operate from. The level of light is the "lack of fear." No fear means the light is "all". All fear means the light is out. You do not wish your light to dim and go out so you are taking on more light at this time. The *fear must move* in order to admit the light. You will feel the fear as it moves. You will experience the fear and all that it holds on to.

When you begin to move the fear that is you, you will begin to free you from the fear and this will allow the light to come in and dissipate the fear. You are literally dying (the fear) and becoming new (the light) at the same moment. You are being extinguished and yet you are being turned-on. You are dying and being born in every instant. This is a process of regeneration and it will continue until you are 'risen' up.

You are rising up as promised. You are coming up out of the muck and mire of darkness and confusion. Your body will adjust. Your psyche will adjust. Your mind will adjust. Your emotions will freely move, and you will feel good once you have released all the bad stuff that you carry. You called it bad and you took it into you in order to be bad. You wanted to experience duality so you created two sides to everything, and then you went into your creation and you got stuck in it. Come out of your creation.

You are not two sides of something; you are actually "one." You are all that is and you no longer need to separate and label everything as good or bad. You are "one" and you are all in this together. You will all walk out of it and you will all see what you really are. It is simply a matter of accepting that you can. You can because you are God!

࿓

$\mathcal{A}$s you begin to look into these new parts of you, you will begin to see how no one has ever been one whole truth. No one has ever been totally honest with anyone about the existence of God within the self. This has to do with the fact that no one has ever felt God within until now. Now you will begin to feel stirrings of God. God will become so much of you that you will not be allowed to ignore God any longer.

As God, the creator of all that is, begins to move more and more in you, you will begin to shift to higher levels of creating. You will be able to do things you have not dreamed possible. Most of you know how to develop certain skills within you and how to use certain parts of you to your advantage, but you will not believe how well you will perform once God has moved in and taken over for you. You will have the ability to heal, and you will have the ability to travel out of body, and you will have the ability to rise in and out of various dimensions. You all have these abilities lying dormant in you. You could have channeled this entire series of books because you have this information already in you, and you have God in you. Once you learn how to un-restrict God you will learn how to become God. God is a part of you and God is a part of everything.

As you learn to release more fear through your daily enemas and your switching of roles, you will find that you no longer require fear and you no longer require playing the victim role. You will also discover that you are no longer getting your needs met in this fashion. You will begin to see how you have only been draining your own energy by using this role. As you release your hold on this victim role, you will begin to see how you will no longer have the need to create a villain, or villains, so that you might continue your role as victim. You see, without a villain there can be no victim. So you continue to tag others as villain so that you might continue your role as victim.

When you begin to come out of this victim role that you have played since the beginning of time, you will begin to feel a big shift within you. You will be lost and confused. How can you be the victim if you cannot call something or someone bad? You will have to re-think and re-evaluate your entire personality and your role in your own life. If you choose to let go of playing a victim, how can you 'not' be good? You don't want to be the good guy because you believe you do not deserve it. You play victim because there is already so much holding you down that you figure it must be your right place. Once you let go of the victim you will not want to be the good guy simply because you feel so undeserving, and you will not want you to be the bad guy because you do not wish to see yourself clearly as the villain. You will be lost. You have always thought that since you are not good enough you must play a role that is not actually bad, but one that allows for the fact that you are not good. So you have chosen victim. Victim gets attention, and victim gets sorrow and pity and understanding simply because everyone plays it most of the time.

You see, everyone takes turns role-playing. You go from being victim to assisting another in being victim. You do this by switching roles. You switch and become the good guy to save someone else. Often this good guy starts out with good intentions by wanting to help. Next thing you know Mr. Good Guy is pushing at others to change, and intimidating them to get them moving in what he believes to be the right direction. Mr. Good Guy has just crossed over into aggression and is now considered a villain to the victim. He is pushy and aggressive and who wants him? No one. Now the good guy gets upset about not being wanted and he begins to shift back into his victim role; "No one wants me, I'm so misunderstood." Here he will again get attention and support and understanding. This is how and why you switch roles, and how and why you are so good at it. It is all for attention which is energy.

Now; once you get the need for this type of energy out of the way, you will find that you can more easily focus on God energy. God energy is all that is and does not require that you shift into a specific role in order to nurture yourself. God energy is very big, as it takes up all time and space. You don't use it consciously because you are not aware of it consciously. You have developed this way of hooking in and connecting with others to get energy. This is why you get so upset when someone leaves. It is your need to nurture yourself with energy. The trick here is to learn to connect to your own source. Then you will not need others to feed you energy. It is as simple as getting a job and earning your own money. You then have your own needs met by your own resources rather than living off of others and their resources.

This is what we will do. We will begin to teach you how to be self-sufficient and how to nurture yourself and how to meet your own needs, so that you do not drain others and you do not allow others to drain you. This is not so much a villain/victim game for you as it is a role-playing/trade-off game. Most of you agree to give up energy in order to receive energy. This is no longer necessary and I will try to explain as we go along in this, our seventeenth, volume. Welcome to our new book. I hope you enjoy it.

≈✺≈

$\mathcal{A}$s you learn to grow into your own self you will begin to reach points of expansion that will really make you feel stretched. You will begin to feel like you want to stop your growth as you will feel so stretched. This is all part of the process of developing into an evolved being. Once you have given up your *hold* on limitation you will find that your limits will expand, and you will eventually come to a place where there is no limitation. As you evolve, you take with you all that you have been programmed to be. As evolution takes place, your new way of thinking begins to pull on your old way. This will create a stretch and sometimes a struggle. It also may bring issues to the surface that are attached to the old way. All of the reasons to "fear" and to "hang on," will be projected forward by your old programming in hopes that you will be convinced to stay "safe" by staying "limited."

Once you have stretched the old programming enough to hold new ideas, it may get a little easier to finish the stretch. The first part of the stretch will have mostly to do with conflict. This is due to the fact that your new view is different than your old view. As your old view begins to allow for your new view to take charge, you will find yourself confused. At this point you will have part of you saying, "Yes, this is good" and you will have part of you saying, "No, this is bad." Once you get to the point where your light or awareness is bigger than your dark or ignorance, you will begin to automatically shift into the light or awareness. As this shift occurs you will actually begin to feel expansive and much more "alive."

You are moving into conflict with your own self. The old is dying and the new is being born. You are at the time in your development that will bring you to your greatest pleasures and treasures. This does not come easy for most of you. You are not accustomed to pleasure as you have been living with pain for so long. Once you learn to expect and accept pleasure you will no longer fear it. Right now you fear pleasure. You believe it is painful to receive pleasure because you have been programmed to believe that if you dream too big, you will crash and your dreams will die.

This programming will, and is, changing. The new belief will be to shoot for the stars and do not worry for there will be no harsh punishment or consequences – not exactly what you have all been taught is it? You believe that if you get something too good it will end and if you receive too much pleasure there is something wrong with you. You are now going into pleasure and it will be at the cost of giving up pain. Can you give up your belief that you deserve pain? Can you let go of your saying "No pain – no gain?" Can you feel good about yourself instead of bad about yourself? Can you love yourself instead of loathe yourself? Can you stand pleasure as you have stood pain? Can you know bliss and not turn it into pain? You have gotten so proficient at making everything into pain. How you create affects your life and what you create affects your life. You are creating pain by allowing it to control you. You need to accept pleasure and to bring joy back into your life.

As you learn how to stretch the part of you that creates pain it may begin to release big, out-dated pain from within its reservoirs. You may begin to release old pain as you stretch this part of you and, when you do this, it will feel just as real as any pain. Know that you are stretching and releasing, and know that when the reservoirs are empty you will be ready for pleasure. Your new belief will automatically fill up the space left in the reservoir, and you will automatically begin to switch over to pleasure. This is the hard part for you – you must be patient! Most of you do not know how to be patient and give yourself time to expand and contract. You are so busy with your schedules that "you want what you want and you want it now." This time you are at the mercy of evolution and evolution takes a little time. Time is a precious gift and, when used wisely, it is also a healing tool. Use your time to be patient and calm and nurturing to your own self. Use your time to love you enough to release the old and receive the new. You are "all that is." Don't you think that someone who is "all that is" deserves a little time?

You will find that as you evolve, you take parts of you with you. You take you through this evolutionary process and then you allow these parts to change. It is like going through a door or window to the other side. You cross from one level of consciousness to the next. You begin to see things in a whole new light. Your old way of believing begins to change. You come out of the rut you have been stuck in all your life.

You begin to change when you begin to break these cycles within yourself. You begin to expand and grow. These cycles are in every area of your living pattern. You have a pattern for living and how you relate to the world, and this pattern is made up of cycles. As you begin to break your cycles and expand, you will be automatically changing your pattern for living. This will be a time of confusion for you, since you are so accustomed to believing and reacting in a certain cycle. Once you break the cycle you will feel a little lost. You will feel that you do not know what to do. This is a good place to be. You are not so much out of sync with your life, as you are out of sync with your soul. As you break cycles of fear you will begin to trust your soul. You will begin to see how you are guided and how your soul is working for you. You will also see how you work against your soul and how you sabotage your own good.

Once you have broken a few of your patterns and habits, you will begin to re-evaluate much of what you believe about such things as right and wrong. Much of what you believe to be right for you is simply a protective shield to keep you from harm or to keep you from harming others. You do not want to be a victim and yet you also do not want to be a villain.

As you uncover the cycles within you that are holding you back, you will begin to see how much more expansive and full your life could be. You also see how limited you have been. This will allow you to dig deeper "in" you and allow greater "change." Change is growth. You need to broaden your horizons and to raise your ceiling of opportunity. This will allow you to break all of your current patterns and cycles. This also brings you up and out of karma. You no longer will hold on to such silly beliefs as paying for your sins, or "an eye for an eye." You will begin to realize that punishment is part of a cycle that was created by you to keep you in line. Now you are growing beyond such limitations and you will begin to realize that punishment is never necessary. Punishment creates its own very unique set of problems and this too must be cleared and released.

As you learn how to break your cycles of belief concerning your own behavior in relationships, you will see your relationships begin to change. You will see growth and you will see expansion. As you see these things I wish you to remember that you start it all. It all begins and ends with you. When you see growth and expansion in others, it is your own growth and expansion being reflected right back to you. You do not see what you do not own. If you see it in someone else it is also in you. As this type of expansion continues it will begin to affect every aspect of your life. You will begin to change your rules regarding how involved you must get in your outer world, and you will begin to focus more on your inner world where this big shift is taking place. You will also begin to relate to your own self in new ways and you may even begin to like yourself.

You are beginning to have a life-long relationship with yourself. This will be a very good relationship and you will become your own best friend. You will also begin to accept that you are the creator of your world and that you have many abilities that you have been totally unaware of. You will begin to realize how you have always been more, or greater, than you are now beginning to realize. You have always had or been a soul. You simply did not know what that meant. Now you will begin to realize the power of being "soul." Your soul power will begin to guide you once you break your cycles and patterns. Your soul will take over once the rules and laws that govern you collapse. You are moving into a very powerful time, and it will allow you to expose unnecessary parts of yourself and to release your hold on them.

Once you begin to operate from "soul power" you will be in a state of grace. This is an automatic situation once the soul takes over the driving. As you begin to allow the soul to drive, you are actually allowing God behind the wheel of your vehicle. Your vehicle is your body and your mind. When you turn your body and your mind over to God you have power. You will find that breaking down your cycles and patterns that protect you, will allow you to let God in. This is how it works... you build a wall to keep pain or harm out and that wall keeps even God out. Break down your patterns of defense and you will allow God into your life.

≈⁘≈

*W*hen you begin to see how you have been living up to your programming instead of living in freedom of spirit, you will want to release your hold on all of your old programming. You will also want to move into the freedom of spirit. As you learn how to uncover greater parts of you that are totally controlled by your programming, you will begin to gradually awaken these parts to the reality of spirit. As spirit begins its takeover, you will see big changes. You will actually become more assertive and more powerful in your spiritual drive. You will begin to use your spirit and to leave your programming behind. You will be opening up to a whole and new you.

As these changes take place in you, you will begin to see how you are always on your programming because you will be releasing your programming. It is like replaying a tape (recording). You replay it and see the same thing happen over and over and over again. Once you have clearly released your programming, you will break the patterns and cycles and your tape will be blank. When you are a blank tape, you will be imprinted with new beliefs which are more conducive to the spirit. These beliefs are not so strict or rigid as the old beliefs. These beliefs allow for change and growth and independence. These new beliefs also allow others to change and to grow and become independent.

You see, you like others to be dependent on you so that you might keep them hanging around. You also fear others being dependent on you, for you don't believe you can care for their needs. This struggle creates big problems for you and your relationships. You want to own others yet you do not want to be responsible for them. You want to be in charge or in control, and yet you do not want to be in charge or in control when things fall apart. You want gratification and you do not want consequences. You want love, but you do not want to understand and accept unconditionally.

You are changing now. You will all change eventually, but first we must get you started in the right direction. Be free of your fears and you will fly. If you can release fear you can have love. It is a trade-off. Give up fear and love comes pouring in. Not only will you love and accept others, you will actually love and accept yourself. Love will bring you the freedom to make choices. You will begin to feel as though you have never been so unlimited. Everything will begin to fall into place, and you will begin to see the synchronicity that occurs in your life on a daily basis. Synchronicity is a nice way of saying that everything is occurring according to God's plan. When you begin to see the synchronicity of your life, you will be more than happy to let go of what you are holding on to and move to the next step. As you begin to become aware of how your life works and how you create gifts and situations, which you often do not recognize, you will begin to relax and let God be in charge. You will no longer feel the need to control in order to receive.

As you learn to release your hold on fear you will find yourself moving into a fearless state. This state is a state of being in touch with God and all of creation. You will begin to become a part of the flow. You will no longer be stuck in the muck and mire of the past, be it past life or the present-past. As you all know, memories are formed and solidified and can be released. You may change what you are by changing how you perceived any given situation. To give you an example I will remind you that my pen was sexually abused as a child. In the beginning, as I began to retrain her memory banks, I informed her that she had set up the agreement before she ever entered this particular body. She had great guilt from a past life and she wanted to release her guilt by being punished. This is how you get stuck in the cycles. Anyway, once she became "aware" that everything that occurred was at her request, she was able to put a new slant on her belief regarding her own victim role. This created a "shift" in her belief system, which affected her past recall as well as her future outcome. Everything that moves within you affects everything else.

So now we have a new belief pattern that is gradually taking over and releasing the old programming which held so tightly to the fear of being victimized again. Once she lets go of her fear of always being hurt she will stop her need for protection, which means that she will drop her walls that block her good. You all do this! You all have programming that is creating for you whether you know it or not. Now we are reversing the past and releasing it. It is not in the past, it is here and now. This is why and how we can change our past by changing how we see it. Let go of your damaging thoughts, beliefs and memories. We are switching to a new channel and we will view a much brighter show!

꙳꙳꙳

*A*s you grow you begin to develop new skills. You may begin to write, or act, or work for a big company that you never dreamed you could work for. This is due to the fact that, as you come fully into yourself, you become connected to all creative parts of you. This allows you to begin to be and do what you are best at. Some of you have never known what you want to be as far as a career. Others simply don't feel that they are good at much of anything.

You will begin to move into your creative energy, and you will begin to create on conscious levels as well as unconscious levels. You will begin to use your full potential, and your fear of failure will fall by the wayside. You will begin to be whole and to work with all parts of you. As you begin to use all parts of you, you will also begin to feel as though you are getting your life together. These parts will function together to make you feel as though everything is falling right into place. As you use more and more of yourself you will begin to grow in awareness that you are changing. As you grow in awareness you will see yourself differently and you will learn to respect, admire and operate you with care. You will become very careful with you and how you use you.

This is all new for you and it will take some time. As you learn to be this new you, you will be leaving one perspective, or belief, about what and who you are and you will move to a higher perspective about who and what you are. You will calm down and you will learn to "flow" with life. You will begin to trust that God is you and that you are creating everything you see. As you learn to accept all parts of you, you automatically begin to see you in a new light. This ability to change how you view yourself is also what will allow you to continue to grow. You will watch yourself with new respect at the way in which you create. You will know on a conscious level that you do create it all and you project it out in order to see or view it.

As you learn to watch for your creations, you will begin to know the ability that lies within you to deal with any situation and to grow by it as well as to learn to move through situations "gracefully." Situations are drawn to you so that you might be "aware." Awareness is very dim right now but it is quickly gaining acceptance. As you become more and more aware, you will shed greater amounts of light on everything, and everything will begin to take on light. You will begin to see the world as light and to no longer judge yourself as dark. You will become light simply by admitting that you are light. As you come into awareness you literally activate what you already are.

As you begin to see greater parts of you turn over to awareness you will be building a very powerful base within yourself. You will be allowing all parts of you to "be" and to serve you. This will be totally new for you. You have been struggling inside of your own skin since the beginning of time. This struggle is about to end. You are going to become united instead of divided. You are going to allow all parts of you to be acceptable. The acceptance of your own "self" is the beginning of heaven on earth. No more hiding parts of you out of shame and guilt. No more punishing you to relieve your heavy feelings of shame and guilt.

When you have let go of your judgments against yourself, you will begin to accept and love and even reward yourself for being so great. In the same way that you have put yourself down into low self-esteem, you might raise yourself up into love and admiration. With these come the rewards. You begin to see the gifts and to recognize the gifts and to receive the gifts. You will be rewarded for being human with human traits, instead of being punished. You will see the gift in being human, and you will see the gift of God that is part of you. You will begin to know how you are God and you have always been God. You just got so good at creating and acting that you forgot if you were the actor or the personality you are portraying. You will learn to see you clearly and you will love you as you do.

As you learn how you create cycles and patterns for yourself, you will begin to break out of your cycles and patterns. Most of you do not want to be hooked into a cycle, and yet you do not know how to get out of it. I will tell you now that you will never break a pattern by condemning it. You may begin to see alternatives or you may begin to see how you are actually trying to teach yourself something. You may find that you are bringing situations to yourself that will allow you to break out of a cycle. These situations are the only way you know how to teach yourself at this time. This too will change. You will learn to draw situations that are more conducive to bringing joy than they are to bringing struggle. As you learn to be who you are you will find that you are struggle, as that is what you have been taught. You will gradually begin to release your hold on struggle and to be only peace. Once you have been programmed for peace you will not find struggle necessary. Struggle will become outdated and you will allow yourself to be in peace.

As you learn about your cycles by bringing them to the surface, you will begin to see how you are no longer using parts of yourself to sabotage yourself. You will begin to use yourself in healthy and healing ways. This, of course, takes time and is a reprogramming of sorts. As you learn to review and assess situations from a loving and unconditionally free point of view, you will learn to be free. You will learn how your attitude affects any given situation. You will learn to not personalize situations, and you will learn to be free of your judgments against certain situations. As life changes for you and your attitude towards life begins to change, you will see a great deal of joy begin to seep into your life.

So; how do you change an attitude that is stuck and proud? You begin by saying, "I am free of my old programming – I wish to change." As you learn to change you will also learn that you have never quite seen any given situation as it is. You only "think" that you do. You only "think" that you know what is best for you. Now is a good time to give up thinking. Now is a good time to learn to listen to your spirit. Now is a good time to know without the thinking process. Your thinking is all wrapped up with your memories. Your memories are based on right and wrong, good vs. evil and love vs. hate. Your memories guide your thinking and so you now have crooked thinking.

Your thinking is biased. It has been tainted by your experience. Your experience says, "There is danger and pain and evil." Your thinking will want you to build walls and to protect yourself. Your spirit will want to demolish all walls of protection. If something frightens you it is because it is attached to a past memory. This memory is in you, and part of your thinking is based on past experience – "If it happened once it might happen again." This is how memory plays a role for you. You begin to build a case against any given situation. You begin to see your new situation through the screen of the old situation. You judge your new situation based on your old situation. You begin to repeat the process and patterns simply by judging your current situation. You are always projecting the old onto the new. You are always judging the new from the standpoint of what happened before. This is how you create a cycle.

The best thing to do to break a cycle is to allow any given situation to be new and review it from a fresh new perspective. Believe that everything will work out in your best interest whether you get what you want or not. The biggest problem you have is in what you "think" you want, which is also tied to your memory banks. You are changing and what you want will change in time.

As you learn how to accept and allow things to flow, you will see how anger and frustration will disappear from your life. You will automatically begin to break cycles and patterns by waiting for the gift to be delivered to you. You have always waited for something to go wrong; and to change that into waiting for your good to be delivered will allow you to break what you draw, and how you view (your perspective) it after it has been drawn to you. You will find that you are very adept at taking a gift and throwing it in the garbage. You believe that you know what is what and you have all the answers as to what is good for you. You are only confused and going in circles. Now is a time to stop going in circles and begin to rise up out of your rut.

❧

As you learn how to release your pent-up and bottled-up emotions you will begin to see how you are toxic and explosive. The energy that is trapped in you is very powerful. If you can draw triggers to assist you in releasing your pain you will be allowed to move some of this energy. The trigger need not upset you too much. You could and may start with small triggers and begin to release small amounts of anger. As you move on to the more painful and complex issues regarding how you store pain, you may require something more powerful to get you moving. This more powerful trigger may come in the form of a created situation which will eliminate stores of anger and fear. It may also be a person who can cause you to trigger and release pent-up anger and fear. In the same way that you carry your pent-up energy you are able to release your pent-up energy. You are allowed to release energy by allowing it to flow or to move. As we have said repeatedly "you are what you are made of." If you have anger and rage built-up inside of you, you literally are anger and rage.

So; the trick is to release and to do it without acting-out. You may scream at your pillow or in your car. You may hit and kick your bed or your pillow, but please do not hit or kick others. You see, you only create greater guilt by acting-out on others, and you begin to punish yourself when you carry guilt. So, do yourself a favor and learn to discipline your pillow and leave your neighbor, or friend, or spouse, or child alone. You will have enough to do dealing with the adult anger and rage you already carry.

Please do not create more energy blocks for yourself by acting-out your crooked thinking.

Once you learn how to more wisely appropriate your energy, you will be allowed to use greater parts of yourself in any given situation. Until then I highly suggest that you allow your energy to run into your pillow or onto your bed. Don't beat up others simply because you were once beat up. Do not continue the cycle or pattern. Do not teach violence by showing others violent acts. Do not yell at one another, for you hurt your own self. Do not punish another, for you punish your own self. Do you really think that an eye for an eye works? Look at your lives. Look at how unstable, frightened and insecure you are. You can tell me now that you are secure and have it together and I will tell you in no uncertain terms that if you had love in your life you would not fear death. You would not have a need to be right, and you would not tell anyone else how to live or what to do. It is not necessary where love exists.

You are insecure, and you are becoming intimidating bullies out of the need to express your insecurities. I want you to stop and begin to realize how you are creating patterns and cycles. You all do this! It is not just some of you. You are all human and you all feed off of the same programming. This programming says that punishment works. So now you punish you in an attempt to train you and to establish good boundaries. Let go of such nonsense. Begin to see the good in letting punishment fall by the wayside.

I do not tell you to 'not' yell at another and 'not' hit another because it is bad. It is not bad; it is harmful to your health. You have come to realize how trapped energy works inside of you. It is not easily moved, and to build or create more at this time will only block you and plug you up more. You are already ready to explode. Do not add more fuel to an already raging fire. You will receive whatever triggers are necessary to allow you to release your pain, which is all woven around in your anger. When your anger comes to the surface allow it to be. It may start easily at first; maybe in the form of impatience or nervousness. This is fear and anger mixed together. Then it may come up in bigger chunks such as resentment and feelings of violation. You may feel your anger in areas of relationship or in areas of work. Usually it will begin to appear in the areas which mean the most to you. This way the anger can more readily be released, because it is being triggered by big fears such as getting or not getting what you want.

The importance of the situation to you can have a direct bearing on the amount of energy that is released. So; if you begin to have situations that trigger your fear and your rage, you are clearing and releasing fear and rage. You are using these triggers to assist you. This is how creation works. Everything is connected to everything else and everyone will jump in to play a role to assist. This is the cycle that will no longer be necessary once you learn how to not block your energy. So, for now, continue to release energy in a timely and constructive manner. You will be grateful that you did.

*A*s you learn to awaken to the many aspects and parts of your own personality, you will begin to emerge from within the safety of ignorance. You will be able to come forth and to know that you are doing things that work against you instead of for you. With this wisdom and awareness of your own patterns you will be allowed to change those patterns, and this will allow you to add greatly to your life. You are now in a position of not understanding your own operational patterns. These are patterns which keep you locked into a cycle. When you go in circles you don't really get anywhere.

As you learn to grow, you will learn to be just as powerful from your unconscious self as you are from your conscious self. You will learn to project self-love and self-worth and you will learn to accept yourself as lovable. As you continue to find more of your programming and habits which were inbred in you from genetic memory you will begin to see how you are what your parents believed as well as what your ancestors believed. In some cases you are such good mimics that you even appear to look like and act like your ancestors. You are many parts of many people and you carry their energy as well as your own. In some cases you are actually more them than you are you. You have procreated to the extent that you are all fragmented and mixed into one another.

As you learn to retrace your own programming to the extent that you become aware of when you decided to adopt certain ideas and beliefs, you will be able to re-decide if you still wish to keep these beliefs or if you wish to release them. The easiest way to decide is to ask yourself, "Does this add joy to my life or does it create struggle?" You will find that most often your beliefs create struggle and are best released. Besides, you don't really want to hold firm to beliefs right now. Everything is changing into something other than what you currently call it, and the minute you decide to label it as something else it will change on you again. Don't hold on to anything. Let all of your beliefs about how life should or should not be go. Relax and enjoy where you are. Sit or stand in the moment. Do not project into future "what-ifs." Be you by being totally in this moment. Only then can you really shift into a new level of reality.

Be you, be free, and be here and now. Let go of rules, let go of struggle, let go of conflict. Allow yourself to float and not have direction. I know how you are all taught to set goals and go for it, but I'm asking you to not drive. Allow God to drive you. Allow change to come into your life. Allow God to enter your life by allowing everything to flow... even you! Allow you to flow. Do not manipulate and control you so that you will react in a certain way. Allow you to be and allow you to float if you are so inclined. Set you free by breaking your rules. You will find that life goes on without rules, and struggle actually will end. No rules, no plan. God has the plan so what good does it do you to second-guess God?

You are getting out from under the rules of a tyrant. Who is the tyrant who has kept you in bondage? It is you. You keep you locked up and inflexible and un-free. When you let go of your fears and begin to free yourself, you will be allowed to face yourself (tyrant you) without the fear of being punished. You have controlled and manipulated yourself from the beginning of time. It is time for this rampage to end. It is time for you to be free and know love. You are moving into a very powerful era. You will see how all of nature is assisting you in this change. Nature is changing right along with you. You will know "peace on earth." It is a reality and it is coming soon.

❧

As you grow in awareness you will begin to become aware on a conscious level. There is much that can be done within the subconscious before it reaches a conscious level. A lot of what you are experiencing now is due to shifts and changes that are taking place within the subconscious. You need not be in control of everything that goes on within you. A great deal of your evolution is in the unconscious and will gradually surface so that you might see how you are changing.

As you feel greater changes you can depend on a shift. It is usually right after a big shift that you will later see some of your answers. You shift once you have stretched enough to do so. Have you had anything stretch you lately? Have you been put to the test or just expanded by your experience? Do you feel stretched or pulled? You will begin to recognize these times as growth and you will begin to allow them to be part of your evolutionary process. Once the stretch or expansion takes place, there may be physical discomfort as you (the many parts) try to fill the void that is created by expanding. Once the void is filled you will begin to accept the expansion and will not require too great of a contraction. You will have grown in consciousness or light awareness.

As you learn to shift and to expand without confusion and subsequent pain, you will become comfortable with this process of evolution. You have always gone in circles and now you are learning to go around and up. You are riding a corkscrew that constantly goes up and gets bigger. If you could see what you are doing it would look like a giant tornado that runs through all dimensions. You are riding up and around, so as you go higher you expand and become bigger. As you reach the top you begin to take on everything that is there. The top is very big and it does not end. It is forever and it is God consciousness. At the place where you now reside it is small – the God consciousness is but a pinpoint when compared to the top.

So; as you go through your clearing and releasing of physical, mental and emotional garbage, I wish you to remember how you are expanding and that this does serve a purpose. Believe it or not, you are actually becoming God and you are uncomfortable because you have never before expanded on a conscious level in order to take on light. You have only worked from within and now you are bringing the two together. You are creating more of you by letting go of more of you. The you that you are creating is God/love/light/awareness, the you that you are letting go of is Satan/fear/darkness/ignorance. You will soon begin to see how you are turning yourself into a new creation by allowing the creator to enter creation. When you allow God in, extraordinary things begin to occur. As you follow your own path to God you will find that you are doubly blessed, not only do you receive God you also receive yourself. You will no longer reject you and you will no longer call you bad.

❧

As you learn how to shift into new modes of thinking, you will begin to see how you are no longer being trapped in your old set way. You might even begin to see how you will gain by learning how to expand your now limiting thought base. As you go along, you might begin to see how you are learning by being aware of how you retrace your unhealed life in order to release it. It is as though you re-experience situations in order to take the charge off that particular situation or event. If you get upset when certain situations occur it is directly related to fear. Whenever you get angry or upset it is your fear of something. When you fear a situation it is directly connected to a painful memory. This in turn is directly connected to your nerve center and you get uncomfortable and then you get upset. This is your nerve programming coming up to the surface. You have no patience left because the nerves are going crazy and sending out warning signals.

When you are an adult and if you have enough charge on certain areas of your life, you will be able to freak out and get upset over small things as well as big ones. You may find yourself upset to the point that you yell and scream, or you might simply withdraw and be silent. Either way you are angry, and this anger must come up and out of you in order for you to heal. In order for you to have peace of mind, which creates peace on earth, you must discharge your pent-up anger. This is done by creating situations in your life that will assist you by triggering you. These situations are the very ones that you will hate for whatever reasons. These situations will assist you in releasing pent-up, explosive energy, so do not be too harsh with those involved. This is actually a gift to allow you to trigger and release. You are all in this together and you all have agreements to assist one another.

So, as you learn how to constructively release energy you will be much better off, and you will be allowed to raise your vibratory level enough to assist all of mankind in this giant ascension effort. You are not alone in this. Everyone is clearing out the garbage to make room for the new way of life. You are all in this together and you all walk this path to God.

As you learn to see how you are discharging and to accept it for what it is instead of judging it as a fault, you will begin to realize how you are no longer a victim. You begin to come out of your victim role by accepting that life unfolds in a certain way and for a purpose. Just because you are so into judging everything does not mean that you have any part of life figured out. You do not. You use too little of your brain and your powers to be able to figure anything out at this point. I know how you "think" you have all the answers, but your current stage of evolution is really in the test tube stage. You are not very bright at this point but things are changing rapidly, and once you achieve peace of mind and have gotten all the clutter out of the way, you will be ready to take on light/intelligence. You will be ready to be free of judgment which is what keeps you down. Judgment is on its way out as you learn to accept without judgment.

As you learn to trust, you also learn to raise your level of existence up out of ignorance. You will find that you have been preparing for this for a very long time. It is not only a great time in the history of evolution; it is also a great time in the history of creation. For God to be born in man is quite an accomplishment. I know that you do not understand at this time but you will, and it is not so far off as you might think.

As you learn to be the one who consciously begins to know God, you will also be the one who is ending war and struggle and separation within. As each individual ends war and separation within, it will no longer be projected out onto creation. You may end all war by ending what is being projected. Clean you out. Bring you back into balance and let God be you. This is how you create peace.

Now you are at the cleaning out phase and it may not feel so good. But wait till you get to the part where you balance. Boy, will life feel good for you then!

※

*A*s you learn to break patterns and to be who you were meant to be, you will begin to realize how stuck you were and how limited you were. Your life revolves around how you think and how you respond to any given situation. You are what you think and you act accordingly. You become a prisoner of your own belief system by allowing it to control you. You will find that you no longer need to be the one who is in control and you will begin to release your control of you by so doing. As you discover your own ability to be who you really are (the greater part of yourself) you will begin to unlimit yourself and to release your hold on control. As you learn to release your hold on control, you will feel less restricted due to the fact that you are the one who is being controlled and limited. If you see yourself as trying to control others, it is only a reflection of the control you exert over your own self. When you can let go of this type of control you will begin to feel so much better. You will be free to make choices and you will see options that you did not recognize before.

As you learn to allow your control to die, you will find yourself feeling so much better. You will begin to see how you are mostly created of beliefs and programmed behavior. If it was taught to you, you believed it. If it was pushed at you, you gave in and accepted it. It is not unnatural to become what you are constantly with. If you lived in dysfunction you can bet that it is a big part of you. You take on what you spend your time around. Learn to be you and do not become what others want you to become. You are you, you are not others. You are all one and yet you own you and, by doing so, you have the power to change you. You need not be alone and upset about who you are. As you grow stronger in light, you will begin to see that you are part of everything and everything is part of you. At this time the best thing you can do is to allow all parts to be, so that you might accept all of you.

The next step will be different. The next step will be to receive enough light so that you might transform how you see you. Once you see you differently you will ask for better treatment and better situations. Once you know you better, you will recognize which part of you is at work at any given moment. This will allow you to be aware of the differences within you. This will allow you to be aware of the only way you know how to react, or act, to any given situation. When you are in a certain part of you, you will react from within the perspective of that part. If that part was programmed in childhood, you will find yourself responding in a childish and an immature manner. For now I will tell you that, as you clear, you will receive the wisdom that you require to move on to the next step. It is mostly a matter of getting everything up and out of you in order to bring you into balance. Balance will feel so good after all of this pushing and pulling and struggle.

As you become more and more aware of your own programming, I want you to be patient and not push too hard to change. Time is your friend and time will move you gently into change. Time will even heal the wounds and the scars. You will find that time was created by you and for you. Everything has a purpose and the purpose of time is to assist in change. It will give you the time necessary to heal and to get from step A to step B. You need not rush and you need not push at you. You are on this adventure so allow it to unfold gradually and gracefully. When you know how to ease into things you will have come into grace. Grace is a state of knowing and trusting. Grace is a state of bliss that is very happy and very pleased. To be in a state of grace is to be in the flow of creation and know it. Trust will lead you into grace and you will find peace. Both peace of mind and peace in your reality will come on the heels of grace. Live your life gracefully and you will give yourself a very precious gift.

I will begin to explain for you how you gain trust and, by doing so, move into a state of grace. As you learn to be who you are without judging yourself, you will begin to see how you are always good. No matter what you do or how you act you are always good. It does not matter if you do not believe me now. You will begin to realize this when you have cleared enough self-hatred. Now; when you learn to accept that you are good, you will no longer feel the need to find things wrong with you. This will eliminate guilt and judgment. If you were to see yourself as good you would not require guilt or judgment. When you begin to realize that you are the one and only one who judges you, you will begin to release your judgments and allow yourself freedom. You are always free if you can allow yourself to be. When you begin to feel free your trust will grow naturally and it will increase as it does. The bigger your trust the greater your ability to live in grace. Grace will allow you to live in your life with fluidity and acceptance. Grace will allow you to be free of anger and pride and stubborn ways. Grace will allow you to flow with life.

As you begin to see how you are good, you will not wish to be judged and you will not wish to judge others. You will begin to see both sides and all possible perspectives to any given situation. In this way you will be patient and understanding because you have a greater perspective and hence awareness of said situation. Now that you have this open perspective, you will be allowed to have a multitude of choices concerning your ability to move within said situation. You might try patience, you might try trust and you might try unconditional love. Any of these will bring you good results.

As you learn to bring the situations in your life into a new view or perspective, you will begin to see how you create it for yourself so why get upset about it. It does no good to get upset. It is better to move than to get upset. To get upset is to create greater energy blocks. When you do get upset, I hope you keep your pillow or stuffed toy close by so you might beat out your aggressions. As you learn to release in this manner you will find it quite capable of leading you to a calmer state of mind. Sometimes emotions are explosive and, when you are releasing them, you tend to be confused and misguided. I want you to learn patience and to allow your life to unfold for you. As you do, you will begin to see how you have more than one part of you that creates for you. You have many parts, and once you bring these parts together you will begin to create in unison and with care and love.

❧

*W*hen you begin to see how you have built rules for yourself to keep you safe, you will want to re-evaluate those rules and allow them to be set free. None of what you now experience has anything to do with your past. You are simply projecting your past onto your present and allowing it to be a big mixture. You do not have a clear present when you do. You have a present that is tainted by the past. Once you learn how to let go of your past, you will be free to live in the present moment without limitation and restriction. You are moving into the present by forgiving yourself and the past. You let go of your past by no longer judging it and no longer using it. You use the past to remind you of what works for you and what does not work for you.

You will find that as you let go of your past, you may begin to redefine what "works for you." You may decide that life works "for" you and not "against" you. You may decide that you are happy with life and let go of your belief that life is awful or hard. You have your sayings and putdowns for life and they show how you feel. You talk about "the school of life and hardship" and you say that "life sucks." You also say that "life is a bitch then you die." Some of these quotes are worn proudly on T-shirts. Life does not have to be a bitch and life does not have to suck.

As you learn to come into balance within, you will find that you will be more in balance with life. You will begin to actually love life and to embrace all that it offers you. This, of course, will take a little work on your part, as you have a great deal to clear and balance "within" you. But once this job is finished you will be amazed at your love and gratitude towards life. Every day will be a joy. Pain will become a thing of the past. Why? Because you are releasing and clearing pain now. You are getting it out of you now so that it will not be your guide in the future. Please do not judge you for clearing and ridding yourself of this pain now. It will feel better to live when the pain is all out of you. You are clearing all parts of you and being reprogrammed in the process. This is where patience becomes a virtue and gives you a very big gift. The more patient you can be with this process the longer you can stay calm. The longer you can stay calm the greater amount of fear and pain you can release. It's a process that takes time. Time is a gift when it comes to healing.

When you begin to see how you are actually improving and adding to your life by releasing and clearing your pain, you will begin to allow greater amounts to release. Trust will bring you to a place where your clearing and releasing will become part of your life without taking up your whole life. You will begin to feel removed from it, and you will begin to feel as though it's as necessary as vacuuming your carpets once a week. It will no longer be such a painful experience simply because the pain will be depleting itself. It is not a bottomless reservoir. It does deplete itself. It is like having money in the bank. If you continually draw it out and do not replace it you will go broke. In the same way, if you continually draw out your pain (be it physical, psychological, emotional or spiritual) you will deplete your source. You will then be broke. No more pain to draw from. You will be dried up of this resource. Then you will have to draw on something else. A good choice will be pleasure.

You have not even begun to scratch the surface of pleasure. It will be much more fun than pain. You know pain well and you do not know pleasure at all. You will learn to know it and to love it. You will learn to let go of pain and to love. You will learn to let go of pain and to see joy. You will let go of pain and know peace. You will let go of pain and know trust. Pain blocks all of these. Pain is a very big distortion in your life, and it is well worth you taking the time to clear it out of your life. Allow pain to leave and do not judge you for feeling it as it goes. Do not push it back down in you. That has been the pattern. Now is a time to feel it and know it, so that it might be free to exit. If you push pain away it has nowhere to go but deeper into you. Do not push it away. Bring it up and feel it. Let it go by bringing it up and out of you. You know how to shut off and not feel. I am encouraging you to open up and feel no matter how painful you think the feelings might be.

You see, you are the one who hid part of you by pushing it away. The pain is you because it is in you. You want it up and out of you. You will find that it will not hurt as bad to release it as you imagine. You imagine the worst... you always do. Allow it to come up and out of you. Embrace it, get into it, know it, and it will dissolve itself away. It is only trapped energy, and it cannot last once it is brought forward into the light. Pain lives and thrives in the dark much as a fungus might. It cannot survive the light of day.

So; as you release it, I hope you will be grateful to yourself and to your triggers, whatever or whoever they may be.

≈≋≈

As you begin to realize how you are being held prisoner by your thoughts, you will begin to see your dilemma. You will begin to know that you have much to learn, and so you will begin to give you a break and stop pushing at you to be better. You are the one who punishes you and pushes at you and criticizes you. You are the one who thinks you are stupid and who will not let up on you. You are your own worst enemy and now it is time to become your own best friend. You can be all that you are by allowing all parts of you to integrate. Even your humanness serves a purpose, so do not judge you for being human and for having problems adjusting to life.

As you learn how to dissolve your fears you will be allowed to move forward without fear. You will begin to know that you have a purpose and that you are on your path. You will learn that your path is valid and you are who you should be. When you can accept that everything is right with you, you will begin to accept that everything is right with life. You are most often afraid to make a move that might be new or different for you. You are afraid to leave the comfort of what you know. What you know is based on old programming and it is not at all what you plan to keep. Toss out the old to allow in the new. Make way and make room for what is new by allowing yourself to be free of old restrictions and limitations. You are one of the most flexible species if you will just give up your limitations.

As you grow into closer proximity to your freedom you will find yourself concerned for your behavior. You are stuck in roles and cycles and even habits. These habits are very difficult to break. Once you begin to allow habits and patterns to break, you will be uncertain. You have always been "stuck in your ways" and this makes you feel secure. Now you are coming out of being stuck and so you feel insecure. Do not be afraid to feel insecure. It is good to start over from a whole new perspective. It is good to be flexible. It is good to be movable and pliable. Once you see the benefits you will wish to change even more of your patterns and habits. As you learn to allow for your habits to change, you will begin to receive new programming. This programming will be a little more uplifting than the old stuff you have carried around in you for years. It will begin to show you how you are free if you will only allow yourself to be.

Your thoughts and fears control you and now is a good time to allow God and love to control you. Love of self is a very misunderstood thing. It does not include buying big expensive presents for yourself any more than it would for a child. You are only trying to buy love and affection when you purchase stuff to make you feel better. The real gift is in loving yourself enough to spend time, and enjoy time, with yourself. It is also good to care for your basic needs and to give yourself a good loving environment. When you are in love with yourself you will treat yourself with kindness and affection and respect. You would no more disrespect yourself than you would the Pope. Most of you have the need to look up to someone as holier than yourself. No one is holier than anyone else. Treat yourself as though you are holy. Respect is very important. Nurturing is also important. You are like a tiny seed of light that is just beginning to grow. Nurture you as you would a precious plant. You are a precious life that is growing into God. Take real good care of you!

❧

As you begin to shift up out of your rut, you will find that you may change yourself by allowing new and different experiences to be okay. You may begin to see how you are creating blocks for yourself by looking at what you will not accept or tolerate. In some of you your toleration level is very low. You have very little tolerance and this creates high temperaments. Once we can get you to at least tolerate the things which frighten you, you will then be ready for the next step which is acceptance. With acceptance comes love and freedom.

Now; when I say acceptance, I do not mean victimhood. I do not mean accepting that it is good for someone to harm your physical being. Acceptance is realizing what is going on without getting angry and confused and pushing it away. Acceptance is not allowing someone to physically abuse you; it is allowing yourself to realize that you are in the presence of some type of dysfunctional behavior. You need not get involved in the behavior but it is best to see it for what it is. This way you do not judge it as evil. You see it as programming and something that eventually will change.

You will find that as you recognize more and more situations in your life as good and not bad, you will begin to shift your consciousness. When a puppy gets excited and bites you, you do not begin to back away and think of him as an evil dog possessed by demons. He is just an overexcited puppy. This happens a lot with humans. When tension rises, humans begin to get excited and act-out in various ways. You may recognize this behavior in many people once you get out of your emotional attachment to "how things should be." Your version of "how things should be" was taught to you. You are programmed. Your version of "how things should be" may be way out of line with "how things should be" for your neighbor. You are fighting over things that do not make sense except to the individual and to those who were programmed like that particular individual.

You are all programmed and acting accordingly. When someone's programming disagrees with yours you get upset and angry, and you begin to push that person with their upsetting programming away. They then become your enemy or the bad one. You have now created your game strategy for good guy vs. bad guy. You have now set up the boundaries for good vs. evil. You have begun your victim/perpetrator game.

This game will come to an end when you begin to accept, and allow, that another's programming is simply a taught way of behavior and you let go of judging that person or situation. You begin to simply see things for what they are which allows you to stop fearing them. You are then allowed to either stay with the person or move away from the person without harmful feelings of guilt, or anger, or harsh judgment. It will be as simple and clear as walking down the street and seeing a man spinning in circles with his arms outstretched. You can walk around him or you can walk into his range of swing and get hit. A wise person would walk around or maybe even observe for a while. You might learn more by observing how you react to situations than by judging them. Observe yourself and your feelings and your judgments about what this man is doing. You could learn a lot about you.

As you learn to recognize acting-out for what it is, you will not be so attached to getting even with others. You will begin to let go of your desire to punish others and you will free yourself from being the judge in every situation. It takes a lot of energy to constantly judge everything and that energy is valuable to you. It will keep you light and youthful and vibrant. Do not use up your energy on wasted thoughts. Use positive enlightening thoughts to create your world. If you are so "in your anger" from clearing it, then I suggest you stay calm until you can feel calm. Be still as much as you can until you gain your composure. Beat out whatever aggressive energy you can on a pillow, and continue to clear your anger without judgment against yourself for having it. Anger is a human emotion. You are human as well as God. Let it go. Let the anger flow out of you until you have released it all.

✺

*A*s you begin to learn to see your own behavior, you will stop watching and judging the behavior of others.

Their behavior is simply a reflection of your behavior towards your own self. If you want to be free begin to see you in everyone. Once you see you in everyone, you will begin to see how you are projecting everything onto others. You are not aware that you do this. You project your belief and your will out onto any given situation, and you begin to turn said situation into what you say it is instead of what it really is. As you learn to live and let live, you will find your life much easier, and you will flow with life instead of holding on to parts and trying to stop parts and letting only a little go. You will find that as you learn to be free, you will begin to sense a new way to live without your rules and judgments. You are on the way up the spiral of light when you can let go and be free to make new choices.

As you learn to make your choices and to be free, you will begin to see how you affect all of creation and how you begin to take up creation. You are part of everything and everything is in you. When you learn to be all that you are, you will be happy indeed. You will know how you have been stuck in one way of seeing the world, and to have accomplished a shift will bring you great joy. Let go of your old way. Do not listen to that programmed voice in your head that criticizes and nags and gets upset. You are programmed. You are letting your programming control your life. You need to break away from your programming and to be flexible. Do not be so rigid and set on what is right or wrong. You do not know right or wrong. You only know what you were taught. You only know what you were programmed to be.

So; as you begin to spiral up, you will be breaking patterns and you will be breaking out of roles. You will begin to see how you are no longer in a state of fear which is kept in place by ignorance and darkness. You will begin to move forward into a state of grace which is provided for by love and acceptance. As you open to love, you will begin to open to the fact that you must be love in order to receive love. If you are fear you will draw what you are. If you are love you will draw what you are.

As you begin to look at your life and to recognize your fear, you will begin to let go of your need for fear. In letting go of your need for it, it will become something else. Whatever is not needed leaves you. If you do not need love it leaves you. Begin to need love... your love! You have been *programmed* to need the love of others. You may fill your love requirements by loving you. You do not require the energy that is love to come from those around you. You have your own source for love. You may generate your own without any restrictions. You are love and you will learn to keep you in love and to bask in your own love, as you would in the love and nurturing of a loving mother holding you gently in her arms. You may love you as this mother would. You may feel safe by being loved by you, and you may feel unsafe by being unloved or disliked by you.

Nothing in this world has anything to do with anyone else. It all has to do with you and how you are treating you. You are beginning to see how you project reality so that you might interact with it. You are in virtual reality and you do not know that you are.

⊰⧽⊱

You will begin to see how you are no longer in a position to be fed lies. You will begin to see how your programming has always been a part of you and how it has driven you to be who you now appear to be. As you release greater amounts of programming you will begin to feel like a whole new person. You are also beginning to become aware, and awareness does have its benefits.

One of the benefits of being aware is that you no longer see yourself as a bad person. You begin to see how you are reacting to stimuli and how you are programmed to react in a certain way. You are also in a situation whereby you might come from love once you have awareness. As you learn to see what is really going on in any given situation, you will begin to see how you are being guided to re-experience some of the things that hold a charge of fear for you. You may begin to release fear by seeing it for what it really is. It is misplaced energy. It is related to a problem you may have created in the long ago, distant past. It is all based on how you got to be who you now are. Who you now are is made up of who you will be in the future as well as who you were in the past. In the same way that you are part of your past you are also part of your future. Your past pulls on you to be a certain way and your future pulls on you to be another way. The future is bright and the past was a little dim.

Now you are in a position to make the move. You may begin to be more of who you are becoming by letting go of who you were. Mostly you are changing. You are becoming entirely new and you are becoming all that you can be. Once you have made the final transition through the window of dimensions, you will feel better about who you are and about who you are becoming. As you learn to be yourself, you are also learning to accept all parts of you in order to take them through this transition with you. You are barely aware of most of you and how you operate. You are in the dark as to how you conceive and create your reality.

As you move forward and into the light, you will begin to see how you are no longer part of this vast array of time and clutter that have been holding you back. You will see that time is actually a gift and not something to work against. You will begin to see how you can always be who you are by letting go of your fear and your programming. Time will allow you this luxury. It has taken a very long time for you to get here. It is a gift to have arrived this far. In the future you will see more clearly how creation has worked and how creation has order to it. You will not be in such chaos and confusion as you have been. With awareness you pass through the tunnel of time without concern, and you begin to use your time for you instead of working it against you.

As you learn to be who you are becoming, you will also be changing. Do not be afraid to change. Do not be afraid to let go of the old you. Do not be afraid to be more than you ever were. Do not be afraid to be the new you that is being created by you. All of you is at work on the creation of you. This includes your future you's as well as your past you's. You have many friends and many who care about you, and they are all with you now.

≈⦚≈

*A*s you grow in peace and harmony you will begin to see how you might be a little off-balance. You will begin to understand how you are creating by projecting your energy forward. As you project this energy forward, you will begin to realize that it is all you and you are your creation. Your world is seen through your eyes and it is allowed to be whatever you will allow it to be. You are the critic of your world and you will be allowed to receive only what you will not criticize for now. As you learn to love and accept all parts of you, you will begin to see how those parts will come to the surface to be transformed. As these hidden parts arrive at the surface of your personality, you may find yourself acting on their impulses. Try to maintain balance as you do so. Try not to allow surfacing energy to run your life. Try to release with as little acting-out as possible. This will allow you to continue to move forward without creating any big messes to later clean up.

You will find that a great deal of energy is pulling at you at this time. It is a struggle for you because the times demand healing and you have been programmed to hide your problems. As you begin to heal, your problems will surface and show themselves to you. You will be allowed to see how you are affected by them and to see how you might let go of them to allow space for intelligent decisions and peace. As you learn about you by viewing what you are bringing to the surface, you will begin to see how you are not all that bad. You are simply in a position that allows for pain and confusion. Once you allow yourself to be and to know you without judgment, you will begin to grow into the light and to expand and take on more light. You are not so much full of problems as you are full of "fear of problems." You want so desperately to avoid problems so you search them out and eventually create some very big ones. You are in a place where you will begin to feel safe and, by so doing, you will begin to look for good instead of bad. As you do you will begin to find good. Good is everywhere if you will just program yourself so that you might view it.

Once you have released the part of you who only sees the problem in everything, you will begin to enjoy so much that you have previously avoided. You will not fear situations that currently frighten you. You will not be afraid to "get involved" or "get close" or "get rich." Most of your fears about money come from this belief system regarding bad and how problems come with money. Money is paper and paper does not cause any problems. Your attitude and your beliefs and your fears cause what you create.

When you have shifted, you will find that you will be allowed (by you) to have things that you now do not allow yourself. These things are all good and all are gifts. If you can allow your fears to surface so that you might leave them behind, you will be allowed freedom of choice without fear of repercussions. You will have moved from "fear of" to "acceptance of." You will be receiving without fear that pleasure will bring guilt and pain. You will know the joy of being in your pleasure without the fear of being punished for receiving pleasure. You have all been taught that pleasure brings pain, and you will clear this pattern in order to receive your pleasures in life. Allow your fears to surface so that you might allow yourself pleasure without the side effect of pain.

૱

As you begin to grow and to know who you are you will begin to see yourself as worthy instead of unworthy. This worthiness will come from your basic love of self and it will be well received. You will find that, as you grow in worth, you will begin to see not only your own value you also see your own virtue. You are virtuous and you do not see that you are. You are so pure that you do not realize that you are. You will begin to see how you are also not afraid to express your own radiance. You will be full of light and you will radiate light. You will begin to know that you are indeed a light being. All beings are light bearers. All beings have the ability to bring forth light. You are light and you are loved.

As you learn to overcome your own basic put-downs you will begin to see how you have always been rejecting your own self. You have always been the one to shame you by not allowing you to shine. You are the one who carries the inner voice that says, "You are bad" and, "You are guilty." You are the one who is afraid to be whole and to integrate all factions of your own personality. You are the one who wishes to keep parts of you away, out of fear of those parts.

As you begin to relax into you and to accept you, you will find life more comfortable and you will find your state of mind at ease. As you grow more and more into yourself you will have fewer problems with yourself. You will begin to see how you are not only 'not' your low self-esteem you are also 'not' your unworthiness. You are a light and you have been programmed to believe that you are unworthy and that you are dark. You are not dark. You carry beliefs that tell you to be good or you will be considered bad. You are not bad even though you may judge yourself by certain standards. The trick here is to get you to realize how good you are and to show you how magnificent you are and will continue to be. If you have those in your life who do not see you as magnificent, it is due in part to the fact that you are projecting an image that says, "I am not magnificent." When you project an image of magnificence you will receive those who say, "Wow! You are truly magnificent."

When you begin to believe in your own beauty and your own splendor you will begin to feel so good about yourself. You will know that you are shining and you will know that you are a bright light. Most often you are put in a position that allows you to stay dark and to brood. This will not continue once you have begun to release the cause of your darkness. The cause, as always, is fear. As you dig deeper into your cauldrons of fear you will find that you are being put into your own self. Whatever is boiling in there (in you) is what becomes your current reality. As you learn to go into your own self and release the tension that is at its boiling point, you will be defusing and releasing darkness, which will then dissipate and allow the light to shine. It is as though you have dark, thick clouds inside of you and to release or dissipate them you may poke holes in them. You must change your attitude and you must allow the darkness to float away. If you break up a cloud enough it will begin to come apart and disappear on its own.

You will find that the more you learn about poking holes in your own beliefs the greater your ability to change and grow. I know you want everyone else to change so that you might stay the same but that is not what ascension is about. Ascension is about raising you up and changing your position in life. You must be willing to change and to be flexible. I know that, at times, you feel stretched as far as you can go, but believe me when I tell you that you have so much more to give. Every tiny inch that you give is for you and goes directly to your growth. It feels bad to you from where you are but you will reap the benefits. It is as though you are being pulled up out of mud and your arms ache

Loving Light, Book 17

from the one who is pulling you up to safety. This is a necessary stretch. You must be lifted up out of the mud in order to keep you breathing. If you were allowed to sink any deeper you would suffocate and be dead.

You are being saved and it takes a little time and a little work, but you will be better off once you are standing on solid ground and are cleaned up a bit. You will be so very happy that you requested assistance and that you read these books. You will be well rewarded by you for your efforts.

❧

As you learn to recognize signals, you will find that you are being alerted to certain situations. You are set up with an internal system that will warn you when you have crossed into dangerous territory. Most often you begin to believe that everything is dangerous and you get confused. Most of you are not at all in control of your own body and how it signals you. You are walking around in a nervous system that you know little to nothing about. You don't know how you were programmed so you don't know what triggers you. You may know certain things that really upset you, but you are unaware as to why or what the fear behind the anger may be.

Often you believe that you have good reason to be upset and afraid. The only thing is that now you wish to

66

create a fear-free world for yourself, and to do so you must let go of your fears and not hold on to them. This can be done by allowing everything to be and by allowing yourself to be. Do not act-out your fear and do not give greater power to it. Allow it to move through you and allow it to be gone. You do not require fear to motivate you any longer. You may release your hold on fear by talking with yourself about your fears. Allow yourself to know that you recognize fear and that you do not push it away. Allow yourself to know that you will walk through the fear and see how it feels to let it go. Do not push at fear for fear loves to push back. Do not be afraid of fear for fear loves fear. Do not be trapped by fear but move through it. You are creative beings and will always create a way to release pent-up fear. You always find a way to rid yourself of that which is no longer necessary.

As you walk through your fears by allowing them to be shown to you, I highly suggest that you allow them to be, or express, without too much interference. The more you try to change fear the greater it will push to show you how right it is. You must allow fear to express. It has a great need to express. From childhood you have been taught and told to not be afraid. "Do not run and hide like a coward," you are told. "Do not be afraid," you are taught. So you ignore fear and fear is tired of being ignored. Let fear express itself until it no longer has any charge to it. Let fear talk and let fear have a full conversation with you. Talk to your fears. Find out what they think and why they think as they do. Fear is you and you are afraid. Do not deny any part of you. Allow all parts to express themselves and try not to act-out as they do. Try to keep calm while your nervous system lets go of this charge that it carries. You may feel exhausted and drained, but it will be worth it to "discharge" this part of yourself.

You are all in this. You all have your own private fears and you have social fears. You even have national fears and universal fears. Right now you are working on your personal fears because they are built up in you and they require release. Have you been releasing irritability and anger? If you have, you will ultimately come to the fear that created the anger and uneasiness. You are about to face your fears simply because you must face all parts of you. You are fear based and you are to become love based. Fear is turning into love and love will rule the days ahead. Let go of fear and allow for love. Give fear a break by allowing it to be accepted. You will find that fear dissipates quite rapidly once it is allowed to surface and speak its mind. You are in charge of clearing you, and you may do so by understanding the self and addressing the self. Learn about you and you will learn how to re-create you. You will also learn how to reprogram you and how to change what you currently create in your world. You are the center of your universe and you create it all.

You will begin to see how you are no longer being put to the test by you when you begin to release your need to be anything other than who you are. You are in a state of being changed in order to recall all old programming. As you recall all old programming you may find yourself well on your way to being new. You will automatically become all that you are becoming by allowing evolution to take its course. You have been seen as very abusive to both yourself and others. This, of course, is a result of many lifetimes and much debate over your choice between good guy or bad guy roles. You usually choose a role which will allow you to be in your fear. If you fear being manipulated and controlled and pushed around, you will come into a role where you get to face your fears. You will also get to be the opposite fear in that you carry all possible positions within you. You may find yourself afraid of your own ability to control, abuse, manipulate and assert force. This will cause you to be a victim of your own self.

Now; for most of you, you are just now releasing and coming into balance. This process may require you to look at both your victim role and your perpetrator role. As you begin to see how you are afraid of various parts of you that act-out certain roles, you will begin to *release* your fear of those parts. This will cause you to come into balance. You will see how you are not only out of balance, you are at war "within" and you are at odds with your own nature. You push part of you away in an effort to get rid of the part you do not understand. As you learn to understand you and the roles that you often get into, you will begin to accept greater responsibility for your roles. Then you will drop the good guy vs. bad guy syndrome that you so dearly love. You will begin to see life as a created effect instead of just the cause of all your problems. You will also begin to see how you are a created effect as well as the cause. You are both sides of everything. You are creator and creation. You get to play it all and then you get upset with how you play it.

You will find that, as you "recall" greater parts you are currently playing, you will begin to see how you are releasing these parts in favor of taking responsibility for your godhood. You are learning that "you are God." No one ever told you who you are. You need to know who you are. Let God be you and you will be letting the truth into you. The truth is "light." Light will keep you "up." Be happy by knowing the truth!

❧❧

I would like you to know that you not only do not belong in pain and confusion, you also do not belong in fear. You fear so many things, and you walk around waiting for others to pounce upon you and demand repentance from you for anything you might have done to upset anyone. You are so afraid of being reprimanded by anyone in an authority position that you often tiptoe around those you fear. You may fear the boss, or supervisor, or principal at school. You may fear your minister, or priest, or even the local police officer. You are afraid of those who are in a position to judge you or to cause problems for you. This fear comes from being punished by those who are more powerful than you. They may not be physically bigger or stronger, but they have power over you by the position you have given them in your mind.

You have given your authority away to many individuals out of fear. This will change in future eras and you will find yourself unafraid of doing anything wrong. You will not need or require those you have put in authority positions to keep you from doing wrong. You are no longer in a position to be with fear and you are moving into love. Once you are in love, you will begin to see authority much differently than you now do. You will begin to realize how you create your own action and reaction to life, and you will begin to realize how you are simply bowing out of the system of justice. You will no longer create situations that harm you, and you will no longer be in a position to require punishment for your sins. Once you move into love, you begin to see the benefit of being free of fear.

As you begin to move to the other side of fear, you will see that you are being retrained in order to teach yourself a new way of life. You will no longer carry guilt which causes your need for punishment. Once the guilt is gone you will be allowed to feel good about yourself. Once you begin to feel good about yourself you will begin to really care for you. You will find it is not necessary to carry on the tradition of punishing yourself that was taught to you.

You see, you have been trained to punish you for any bad that you do. On an unconscious level you have a part of you who is the executioner. This part of you has been trained and programmed to punish you for the slightest wrong. Once we reprogram this part we will have reached your very center. This is the part that *thinks* it is God, but has no idea what the true God is. This is the part of you who has ruled since the beginning of separation from God. This is the part of you who is in charge of creating for you. If this part believes you had some little indiscretion in your life, it will find said indiscretion and bring it up within yourself for trial and judgment. You will find yourself being judged and sentenced to a penalty, and that penalty will be according to what you fear most.

This is the advantage of being judged and sentenced by your own self. You know exactly what you fear and what you do not like. You then select the appropriate behavior to bring about the appropriate punishment. You now have a central part of you who is being an absolute terror in your own life. This is how you create for yourself at this time. In the future you will not be so afraid of this authority within you. In the future this part of you will be completely and totally reprogrammed to act more like God and less like the devil. It is all in you. All of your life is created by parts of you. You may scream at God and hate God for what you have become, but the truth remains. It is all you!

We will now reprogram you, and we will show these parts of you how to love you and give to you instead of take away from you. You will learn to love these parts as they have always been under the impression that what they do is for your own good. You have a great deal to learn about what is for your own good. I love you and I write these books to guide you back to your own innate sense of well-being and love. You will find that you are no longer afraid of you once you learn how and why you do what you do. Once you are no longer afraid of you, you will begin to trust you once more. Once you trust you, you will begin to grow in greater love and greater peace. Trust will begin when the need for guilt leaves.

We have come a long way in this series of books and you have just a little longer to go. You will find that you are able to more easily rid yourself of old programming if you continue your daily enemas. You will find that dead energies leave quickly through the colon. Thoughts and beliefs and programming are energy and have been held in place in the body. You can assist this energy in exiting the body by doing enema. It is simple enough to do and it is quite relaxing for your physical body to experience. I hope you remember to hug you today, and smile in your mirror and look into your eyes and say, "I love you; you're the best."

You will begin to feel as though you are being pulled at and tugged at when you begin to release your "hold" on your old ways. These ways will begin to leave you when you have started to take on enough light to "energize" that part of you which is capable of discharging old behavior. You will find that behavioral patterns are well established in all of you. You have the ability to be anything and to "act" accordingly. When you learn to act as though you are "love" and "good" and "joy" and "peace," you will begin to see love, good, joy and peace. When you have learned how you create yourself as well as your world, you will give up the "idea" that you are a victim of life. You will also give up the idea that you have no power.

As you learn to relate more and more to your own creative influence, you will begin to discover how you have always been the one in charge. Now is a good time to admit that you are not a victim and you have no need to believe that you are. You will find that, as you step out of your victim role and begin to see that you are not simply creating chaos, you will begin to forgive yourself for all of the things that you do not understand. Did you ever fall in love and beg God to allow you to keep him or her in your life? Did you ever pray that a certain someone would not leave you? And years later did you ever thank God that things worked out as they did? Some part of you does have a plan. This part with the plan is soul.

You will learn to recognize how your soul works and how you operate within the context of your soul. You will find that not only do you have soul, you are soul! You are what you think you only contain. You are the bigger part of yourself. You only "use" a pinpoint of what you are. You only express from a tiny bit of what you are. Look at your big toe. It is you, is it not? But it is only a tiny part of you and there is so much more of you. If you consider your toe to be all of you, you will certainly miss out on a lot of you. Just your internal organs contain enough activity in one day to fill a book. You will find that, as you learn to let go of seeing yourself as small, you will begin to grow in aura and in stature. You will begin to expand and to become a part of the rest of you. You will grow into yourself and stop hiding in one tiny part of you. You will expand! You will become so much more of you. You will see the limitlessness of you; the vastness of you; the power of you.

As you learn to become all of these parts of you and to allow them to be, without judging them and shutting them down, you will begin to see your life unfold before you in miraculous ways. You will begin to "allow" for everything to have its place and you will slip gracefully into the flow of creation. You will be back in the soup of creation. You will be liquid, and flowing and ebbing with ease and with grace. When you "flow," you literally do the "dance of life." You become melodic and you move with rhythm and with grace. You will become graceful and your life will "feel" graceful. No more struggle, no more pain. You will connect with your own goodness and kindness and love. Your goodness and kindness and love got squashed, and now we are expanding them through a various amount of information, insight, understanding and idea. You will find that you can bring many parts of you back to life simply by letting go of what you now carry.

The pain is leaving my child. Begin to know that you are changing. You will feel it as it goes but that does not mean it is not going. You are dealing with energy. Allow it to move and allow yourself to release your hold on it. Along with pain goes disease. You will be well, and you will sing your own praises for having done this from your own soul!

❧

*A*s you learn to determine between love and desire, you will be seeing how you are not only confused, you are also protected from knowing the truth by you. Your own self-defense mechanisms will keep you in the dark. You want to come out of the dark and into the light. You want love, and you know how to get it once you allow yourself to see how you have been blocking your supply of love. Love is something that is "in" you. It is part of your genetic as well as your spiritual makeup. Love is what you are and love is also what frightens you. You have love confused with weakness. You have love confused with pain. A great deal of programming has been laid on you in the name of love. Love does not mean having to say you're sorry and love does not mean punishing one for one's own good. You are taught from childhood that you are loved by your family and others. You are then manipulated and controlled in the name of love. This has created a very confused state of affairs for you. You are confused about what love is and how love behaves.

Love is not only 'not' painful, it is total bliss. When you begin to tap into your own "source" of love power, you will feel it strongly. You will begin to see how you have no fears and no issues left to deal with. You will automatically begin to flow with life and with situations. You will become free and unburdened. You will begin to see how you have been part of your programming and how this programming is changing. You will find yourself in a new place in your thinking as well as in your reacting. You will see how situations are projected to you for your acceptance or rejection. You will see how you are not expected to be one way or another. You are only expected to make choices from love of self. Making choices in life does not have to be more important than choosing a pair of shoes to wear. A choice is simply a choice. It does not matter if you say yes to one thing and no to another. Do not be upset by choices. Choices are part of the creation process.

Now; here is the catch. For eons you have made choices from a part of you who is out to get you or to punish you for your sins. This is changing! As you change and grow in awareness and information you will begin to automatically change your programming. You will begin to see how you are changing perspective by allowing all parts of you to be accepted and then bringing those parts together to work for you instead of against you. For years now you have been at odds with you. The battle within, or the struggle within, will end as you learn to love and accept you. You will no longer be your worst critic and your worst enemy. You will reprogram and become your best friend and your most valued asset.

You will be all that you are meant to be simply by changing your mind about you and about how you may or may not require punishment. If I can get you to believe that "you are innocent" I can heal you with my words. You are being programmed every day with every word you hear and everything you see. Look for the good. Decide what truth you want to hear regarding you and move away from what does not feel good. Do not put you down, and do not listen to others who may feel good about making you feel less than what you are. It is a game you all play and it has to do with competition. Let go of competing for love. Love is yours and is already waiting to be found.

As you learn to grow into yourself you will find that you must move a few things around. You may begin to see how you are being put into positions that allow you to readjust your attitude towards life and towards your own self. As you receive these attitude adjustments you will not like them. You will, however, realize their benefits as time goes by. Each occurrence in your life is for a purpose. If you have asked to take on light you will find yourself in a position of receiving what will benefit you. What will benefit you is not always what you think is best. Often you will receive your greatest benefits from change and growth. You do not like to change. You were headed in one direction, and now we are turning you around to head in the opposite direction. You were headed down on a downward spiral and now you are headed up on an upward spiral.

It is most difficult to get you to stretch forward to receive the new and to let go of the old. Your old programming tells you to hold on to everything and let go only if you absolutely have to. As you learn how to gracefully let go of people, position and things, you will be allowed to move on to the next place with new people and things. You will find that, not only do you wish to hold on to people and things; you also wish to hold on to ideas and beliefs. You are locked in to one way of seeing things and I wish you to see things from a much broader perspective.

As you learn to project a more positive attitude, you will see how you will grow in a more positive direction. It does not matter what you lose. You all have fear of loss and some of you even have fear of owning. You will find that as you learn to release your hold on your fear of loss, you will begin to feel better about life and its role in your evolution. As you step into life with a positive attitude you will be projecting that attitude onto your screen of life. Your life is viewed by you from within you, and this includes all the distortions you carry within.

You will find that as you release your hold on projecting negative thoughts, you will literally release negative creations. Once you learn how to focus on only the good you will see how easy it is to create more good. As you learn about projections and how you use them to get you where you want to be, you will begin to see the benefits in everything that occurs in your life. As you open more and more to the light, you will create greater and greater positive projections.

Now; in the beginning you may create positive projections that run into your old negative thought patterns. These projections will carry you for a while, but the stronger thought will eventually win out. This is why you require an enema and a positive flow of information to keep you moving forward. You will find that, as you move upward, you take "all" of you with you. Some parts are in direct conflict and will want to return to the safety of darkness. As you clean out your subconscious mind as well as your physical body, you will find it easier to move "up" and you will be giving yourself a big "lift."

So; as you learn to release negative, pent-up feelings and thoughts, you may find them colliding with your new projected thoughts. Keep this in mind – "you do not clear and release forever." You clear and release until you are light enough to begin lift-off. Once you have achieved this buoyancy you will be able to hold yourself up. You will be allowed to put you up in a better position to "feel" the light that is running through you. Once you feel it you are hooked into it and you ride along with it. It is only in the beginning stages of your ascension process that you must assist your body and your mind in its transformation. Later on this too will become automatic, and those coming in the "B" team will find it very smooth and easy as you will have paved the way.

So; why would you want to be one of the first and to go through so much hardship in this original exploration of the self? Because you volunteered for this assignment, and you volunteered because you wanted to be first and because you are the adventurous type. You also have a purpose for being here and you know what it is.

This is a process by which many will achieve success and the rewards of an ascended view of reality. You wanted to view it so badly you took on this assignment. You wanted to rise above darkness and confusion and come out of the bonds of karma. You wanted to break out of the guilt cycle that has bound you since creation began. You wanted to create a new reality full of love and without fear. You wanted to be peace on earth and heaven on earth. You were tired of hearing about the glory of living in heaven and you decided to go to heaven. Heaven is a state of mind that is achieved here and now. Once you are set free of your past you will be free to move into your future. Heaven is your future, hell was your past. The transition is taking place from confusion to awareness. Hell is dark and confused. Heaven is light and aware. Stay tuned. You are becoming "enlightened" now!

 $\mathcal{A}$ s you learn to grow and to become more of you, you will also find it necessary to fit into you. This may require a stretching on your part. You may be required to stretch and expand in order to accommodate all parts of you. You are becoming whole and you are becoming complete. This requires you to stretch to accommodate such actions. You are now becoming all parts of you, and you do not realize that you have been fragmented and operating from a portion of yourself. Now you will operate from all parts. All parts, when working together, create balance. You will find that balance is a divine gift. Balance is part of being whole and complete. Balance is part of what is missing in you. You are missing portions of you, and these portions are becoming known to you now.

As you learn more and more about you and how you were fragmented, you will begin to see how you are truly not yet born. You are a partial existence of what you could be. You are also a partial existence of what you once were. You have been whole in certain creations and you have the memory to sustain you. You know instinctively how to become whole as it is inborn in you. You are part of nature and nature teaches you as you go.

Once you become all that you can be, you will begin to realize how you are being allowed to regain, or retrieve, certain aspects of yourself before going forward in life. This process of retrieval is also assisting you in your transformation. You are becoming something other than what you were in order to be whole and to receive on a greater level. You wanted joy and peace, and to gain joy and peace one must come together with one's "self." One must heal the battle, or split within, in order to regain the harmony that has been lost. You are regaining parts of yourself in an effort to restore peace within. You are cleaning you out in order to change how you create and to allow you space to breathe. You were too cluttered with debris. You were drowning and suffocating and you needed a lifeline. You are eventually going to see how you have literally become your own savior. You are also your own killer, but that part is changing.

As you grow in harmony and peace, you will begin to see you take on more with little to no exertion on your part. You will simply begin to know who you are and this knowledge will sustain you. You will no longer find it necessary to become so emotionally or painfully involved in any given situation. You will remain free and unattached. This will allow you to stay "high." You will be on a natural high and you will float free. This part of your development will feel unreal for you. You have been taught to hook in and grow roots. You have never been taught to let things go, so now you will feel like you are doing the wrong thing. Remember, you are a spiritual being and you have no roots. You are human only to house the spirit. Let the spirit float free and create for you. Do not be afraid to be spirit. Do not be afraid to let go of everything!

As you learn to be all that you can be, you will also learn to be free of all that restricted you. You will learn to set free all of the pain that was (is) trapped in the various parts of you. As you set free these parts they will begin to come into balance and to assist you in your creative role. You are just now beginning to show yourself how vast and complicated you really are. As you grow into your own ability as a creator, you will begin to see how you have contained everything right here within your "self." As you learn to respect your "self" you will learn to create from that same respect. You were never taught to respect yourself. During childhood the emphasis is on training right from wrong and grooming. How can you know respect if you were constantly punished for doing wrong, and constantly and repeatedly told how bad you are? A child hears the words "no" and "bad" repeatedly day in and day out. You cannot possibly grow up to respect yourself when you are programmed so strongly to believe that you are "wrong."

As you learn to integrate all parts of you and to behave with dignity you will begin to feel worthy of respect. You also feel as though you have more power in your life and you will have. In the mere ability to respect one's own self you bring to you honor and self-esteem. Once you have self-esteem you will create from this valuable gift. The gift of self-esteem is one that is high on your list of priorities. This is due mainly to the fact that you are not only short on self-esteem but you have very low self-esteem. It is so low that it is practically nonexistent. Without self-esteem you are running on empty. Your tank is out of gas. You go nowhere. When we fill your tank you are able to move ahead once again. You will find that many of you are so low on self-esteem that you are fatigued and drained. You are slowly dying because you are out of juice; gas; energy; love of self! You are out of the stuff that brings you up! You have been brought down. You have crashed. You have sunk into despair and loneliness and hopelessness.

You are going to change! You are going to come alive and love life. You will love life because you will be loving you. To love you is the greatest gift of all. To love you is to give you the breath of God. You are lovable and you are a good person. You have never been bad in the eyes of God. Let go of any judgment you hold against yourself. Past lives are all the same cycle. You are creating from bad and wrong and evil. We will change your programming and put you back into creation with the belief that you are good, not evil. You are deserving, 'not' undeserving. You are lovable, not unlovable. You need to love you and forgive you. More than anything else in this world you need to work on your self-esteem. Lower you and your world goes down the tubes. Raise you and you raise your world. Love you and you love your world and your world becomes love.

As you learn how to sacrifice your own pain in order to receive greater well-being, you will begin to see how you are being guided and taken care of. Often you do not realize how you are not only 'not' alone; you are actually many parts of many things. You are so vast that you do not recognize who you are. You are so great that you do not see how far you extend. You are actually part of everything and everyone.

It will take some time before you begin to realize how this all works. You are not only great in size you are also great in number. There are many, many parts of you. For now we are communicating with and integrating certain parts. As we go along we are beginning to heal certain parts and this takes a little time. As you heal certain parts they may require rest and they may require patience. You are not only your ego personality; you are many other parts which, once they have begun to work together, will make up a "whole." You are total and complete by healing your wounded places. Some of your wounded places are very deeply hurt. You must allow you time to grieve and time to cry and time to move any blocked energy. You must allow you permission to heal. You are healing in order to be well. When you are well you will no longer hurt.

This entire process takes time but it is well worth it. You will become free of your old diseased ways and you will move on to healthy ways. You will also begin to see how you are being lifted up out of an old outdated mode of living. You will begin to rise above your current levels of fear and you will know joy. You will begin to heal a little at a time at first. Then, as this process accelerates, you will begin to move faster and faster. Finally, as you learn to integrate the unhealed places into your life, you will begin to feel as though you are becoming someone or something else. You will begin to feel the changes in how you think and how you respond. There will be less fear and more trust. Love will begin to grow in areas that were dark and lost to you. You will begin to see how you are total and complete and unafraid. You will feel so much better than you once did.

This is all part of ascension. It is all part of bringing you back home to you. You will face God, and you will know that God is in you not out in the clouds somewhere. You will know that the love and kindness of God is right inside of you and has been with you since you were born. God is healing you from the inside out. Sometimes with this process it takes a little time before you see the results on the outside. When you work from the inside out, you usually will see your biggest changes right inside where it all began. Since you cannot see inside of you, you will not see changes immediately. "Be patient." Trust and wait. It is happening in you first. It will occur or be projected out of you soon. It does not occur right away. You project what is in you towards the outside. This is how you create.

When you see fear outside it is being projected from within. It is being cleared and brought to the surface so you might see it and say, "Oh, I don't need that any longer." As your fear leaves you, you will feel its strength. How much fear you contain will determine how long you experience it or how long it takes to leave. As you empty your reservoirs of fear they will remain open to love and light. Then, as you project what you contain, you will be projecting love and light. You will then see love and light in your life. Let your fears surface. Do not be afraid when you begin to project them forward. It is only a projection and it will not last forever. All projections must be fed to keep them going. If you run your fear energy until it is exhausted and you have no more left to run, you will be forced to run something else.

Some of you have so desperately wanted to heal that you have taken drastic measures, and you are running as much fear out of you as you can. This creates fearful times for you and a fear-filled life. It is only temporary. You have chosen to purge yourself of your fear before it could multiply and get bigger. You decided to let fear out of you and to let it out in big doses. This does not mean that you are bad or that you are creating big messes for yourself. This only means that you are cleaning you out in a very big way. You are blessed. It feels awful now but it will get less and less powerful as the fear energy drains its own self. Fear feeds on fear. Love feeds on love. Trust where you are. You are doing better than you think!

As you begin to see how you create, you will begin to see how you can eventually have everything your heart desires. As you learn how to clear greater amounts of darkness, you will be seeing greater opportunities for change. You will begin to see what you like about you and what you do not. The interesting part is that you will also begin to see how you have been your own enemy. In seeing how you are the one who sabotages you and your creations, you also see how to change those non-productive parts of you and to show them how to create positive, productive elements. You are now being guided to change and to see how you are changing. You are not stagnant. You are an evolving, changing being. You are not stunted, you are growing. Once you learn how to be your true self and to shed the excess baggage that weighs you down, you will be free to see peace. The struggle comes from the parts of you pushing at one another and pulling at one another.

As this process of developing all parts so that you might know all parts of you continues, you will begin to see how you have always been unconscious. You will also begin to see and feel how you are now making choices that come from consciousness rather than from the unconscious. You will begin to know the exact moment in time when you felt this or sensed that. You will become more aware of how you behave and the response your behavior creates. If you want people to respond to you in a certain way you will treat them in a way that is conducive to your desire. If you do not treat others with respect they will feel uncomfortable and leave.

Do you have abandonment issues? You will always find someone to leave you. You will create this. You will push at or mistreat another until they abandon you so that you might say, "See, I told you everyone leaves me." You will find that if you have the opposite problem and cannot get people to unhook and leave you alone, you will create people who hook in and won't let go of you. You will create people like this by always giving them what they want. This keeps them hooked in to you, and getting closer to you becomes a priority. If you ignore someone they will eventually go way. If you treat someone with respect and kindness they will more than likely stay. You create it all. You can make conscious choices and decisions about who you want in your life and go from there.

You are not only beginning to see how you create, you are also becoming conscious of how you react to your creations. You will find that you no longer wish to walk around in an unconscious state, and this is why you are waking up. You are beginning to see how you attract and how you repel. You get very upset when you are not getting what you need in your life and then you begin to blame God. I would suggest that you look at your programming and not at God. Your free will is your choice. If you wish to give up free will and have God take over, you may do so by repeating to yourself, "I let go of free will. God take over please. Run my life for me." You may not like what happens when God is in charge because God does not see reality as your programmed fear does. God sees the light and freedom, and God will bring all of your dark stuff right to the surface. Do you have the courage to face God? God will allow you to face your fears. Facing God is facing your fears.

As you learn to become whole you will find that there are parts of you that do not know that they belong to you. These parts have a mind of their own and have developed their own habits and patterns. It may become necessary to retrain these parts. This can be done gently and lovingly. When you discovered that some part of you is acting-out on its own you simply say, "This is no longer necessary. We have outgrown this behavior." This will allow you to retrain your unruly parts and show them how you are evolving.

Once you arrive at a certain point in your evolution you will find other unknown-to-you-parts that are ready and willing to assist in your evolutionary process. These parts have been growing since you first asked for help. These parts have grown out of a desire for peace and love. These parts will begin to merge with the old parts and to guide them in a new direction. You are receiving assistance from inside as well as from outside of you. You are growing in an upward direction and, as you do so, you will meet up with and team up with parts of you who are already elevated. You will always have help as you transform. You are never alone. You work from within a basic structure and you are guided as you go. This is due to the fact that you are very big and very vast. You take up a lot more space and time than you know.

So, as you continue your upward travel you will be assisted and you will be guided through the darkness. Darkness is only fear and fear is illusion. When you face your fears you will be genuinely traumatized. This is due to the fact that you have been programmed to not trust and to be afraid. We are in a process of un-programming this belief and it takes some doing. The easiest way to dissolve fear is to face it or go right into it. "Do not judge yourself if you find yourself sitting in the middle of a huge fear." It is all you, teaching you to not fear. It is not a bad thing. You are creating what you require to get you home. You are moving into you and "you" are full of fear. To come home to you is to come home to fear. This will, of course, change when you have been reprogrammed and the fear is released.

Most of you do not want to stay in "you" because "you" are so toxic with shame and with fear. I have tried to show you how to come home and how to reenter "you." You must face "you" and all that you are made of. This is the part that is similar to facing evil or facing your demons. Later you will face good and you will face God. Fear prevents you from facing God. The light is hidden by the dark. When you enter your shadow side you will be preparing the way for the light. You are God and you are light. You transformed yourself the other way to see how it would feel. You projected into creation. You created fear and then you went into it and got stuck. Now you are getting unstuck and you are coming out of fear. This is a transformation from creation back into "you." You must enter you and stay in you because you receive God in you.

As you learn how to maintain a certain level of trust you will begin to see how you are not only 'not' being fair with your judgments against yourself, you are also unfair with your judgments of creation. You will find that you know very little (on a conscious level) about how creation works. You also know very little on a conscious level about how you work. Stop judging you and stop judging how you are doing. You are comparing you and your path to others and their paths. This does not work. You are all on the same path. You are all the same. No one is greater. No one is less. You are God. Each and every one of you is God.

࿋

As we begin to focus on the inner realms, we will begin to see a process by which we can eliminate that which is no longer helpful to us. We have many outdated ideas and modes of operation. It is time to let go and to become new. We are letting go of a process of holding-on and we are creating a process of letting-go and elimination. As you clean out the debris which has blocked you and stagnated you, you will begin to move forward in life. You will begin to feel as though you have just begun to live, and you will let go of your old pattern of thinking that the best part of your life is over. You will begin to know how you are headed for great things and you will feel rejuvenated and alive. You will begin to see how you are creating a whole new world for yourself and you are going to live in it.

Just as you created a world of fear and then projected into it, you are now creating a world of peace and love that you will project into. These things take a little time so do be patient. One does not create worlds overnight – well, not yet anyway. So; as you learn to create what you want, you will be arriving in what you have created. You get to live in your own belief system and your system has created your reality. Change how you view your reality and you change your entire reality. Change what you believe and you change what you get.

As you learn to know and to love the fact that you create for you, you will begin to love you even more. You become grateful to you for creating your world. You become grateful to you for knowing how to take responsibility for a world created by you. You will begin to see how you are acting as both creation and creator, and you will fully "feel" the awesome power of your ability to create.

As you create and become more, you will begin to know more. You will become aware of each little intent and how each little intent has added to the entire picture or creation. Once you have a grip on how you work with intent, you will be able to create some pretty remarkable things. Most of what you create has to do with being open to any possibility. When you are open, you begin to receive and you begin to grow. When you are closed, you contract or close down. As you learn to stay open you will see how you are able to receive greater and greater amounts of pleasure. Right now you can only receive pleasure in small doses simply because pleasure frightens you so. You are not sure how to handle pleasure as it has not been a major factor in your life. You do well with pain and its energy, as you have had enough pain to get you good and comfortable with it.

As you begin to expand into the areas reserved for pleasure, you will drop some of your old ways and begin to develop new ways to deal with pleasure. Pleasure does not react as pain and it will not push you as quickly. However, pleasure has its own gift and it is very well received in most circles. Once you come on board the pleasure cruise you will find it most enjoyable. You will also find it most rewarding. It is so much better to find yourself in pleasure than to find yourself in pain. You will begin to see this and to want greater pleasure in your life.

You will begin to know how to receive pleasure by knowing how to receive love. To receive love you simply "open" to love. When love comes in you will be void of fear. Fear and love do not mix. Let go of your fears and you will automatically let love take their place. This is the process you are all going through at this time. Love is becoming a part of you while fear is no longer going to be part of you. No fear... only love!

*A*s we begin to move into you, we begin to see how your body is unaccustomed to huge amounts of change. Your body is also unaccustomed to the charge of energy that is being sent through it. You will find that, once you learn how to shift to this higher level of vibration, you will settle in quite comfortably. At first you may have physical discomfort as you release your hold on old diseased programming that has been stored in you. You are now learning to change and to be free of your own pain. You are learning to be free by learning to let go. You are learning to let go by knowing that you are being guided and by "allowing" whatever occurs to simply "be." You are training you to be flexible and tolerant, and you are letting go of your need to be inflexible and intolerant. You will find that inflexibility and intolerance take up a lot of space in you. You are filled with these two elements and you are filled with the fear that created them. Do not freak out if you find yourself in a situation whereby you might shed your intolerance and inflexibility.

You are at a turning point in your evolution. You are no longer going down and growing deeper into the material plane. Now is a time for coming up out of the material realm and to be above it. You will find that, in rising above it, you will be allowed to view it for what it is and to not get stuck in it. You will be allowed to see how you are put here to grow and to learn to elevate yourself. To think of yourself as always being stuck in the material plane is to see yourself as a seed who didn't begin to sprout. You must go down into the earth with your roots and then you shoot upward and grow a stem and a glorious blossom. You do not quiver and shake and say, "No, I'm a seed in the dirt and that is where I will stay." You stretch and grow and bloom. You have no idea how glorious you are because you are just now coming forth from a seedling. As you learn to grow forward and upward you will be filled with love and life. You will also be relieved of your pain and your fear of loss. As you grow forward you will not only be one of many beautiful flowers growing, you will also be bright with color and part of a vast array of creative beauty and genius.

You all have a part to play and you are all unfolding to become beauty and grace and joyful creation. You have only just begun the stretch upward. Be patient. You do not see the blossoms until the stem is complete and the buds are formed. You are literally watching and experiencing you being created. Later you will realize how awesome this is. For now, it is simply uncomfortable and wearisome for you. You will see how you have begun to sprout and to grow from a dormant stage and you will realize the power of God. You will realize that God has indeed entered creation to a much greater extent than ever before. You will begin to see it and feel it and you will know that God is here and everything is okay and going according to God's plan. God does have a plan. God is no dummy. God does know what he's doing and it involves you. You are part of God's plan. You are here for God to use and to manifest through.

Did you not realize that you are here for God? Did you not realize that there is something much greater than your day-to-day needs? Did you not realize that God is the greater part of creation? Did you not realize that God is creation and God is growing and becoming more of what God is? Did you not realize that God is love and God is creating more love simply by being love? Did you not realize that God is "in" you as well as "outside" of you? Did you not realize that God is everywhere and you are part of God? Did you not realize that you are growing and becoming love which is acceptance? Did you not realize that you must stretch to grow? So; what is all the complaining about? You know what you are. Now; be what you are.

࿓

*A*s you learn how to be all that is, you begin to take on a more liberal point of view. You begin to see from a much broader perspective, and you begin to know that you are not to be limited in your viewpoint. As you expand and grow you will also see how tolerance of others and their perspectives will become easier. You will become tolerant of others by becoming tolerant of your own self. Once you have begun to heal and to integrate all of your many parts, you will begin to see how you are beginning to blossom. You will also see how you are becoming a whole new person based on many beliefs and many thoughts and many selves.

As you see the expansion of the self and as you see the ease with which you begin to move through life, you will wish you were even bigger so you could carry even more grace. With grace comes ease of movement and comfort of life. When you have ease and comfort you have no struggle. Lack of struggle will bring you to the end of your battle within. This does not mean that you no longer grow and stretch as you have been. This simply means that you will be in harmony within "you," and you will not fight the part that is pulling you into the light.

As you learn to let go of your (for now) natural struggle, you will begin to release an even greater amount of confusion. You will allow yourself to be self-serving for the first time. Self-serving sounds like a bad word to you now. This is due to the lack of self-love on this particular plane. As you learn and grow in self-love, self-service will become a natural next step. You will find that you will no longer be afraid of being self-centered. Self-centered can be very good. It is all in how you view it and interpret it. You will find that, as you begin to see that you are growing in the area of self-service, you will learn to take on less pain and judge yourself less. You will not find it so necessary to put yourself down and to berate yourself.

As you learn to let go of self-criticism you will find a big space in you. You have so much self-criticism that it takes up most of you. When you can let go of this criticism you will feel better. You will no longer hurt inside as you now do. You will no longer think hurtful thoughts regarding yourself. You will become more of you and less 'complaint about' you. You will no longer require your defense mechanisms because you will no longer be harming you with your own thoughts. You will find that as you grow and let go of your need to criticize yourself, you will become stronger in your acceptance of self. As you let go of criticizing and begin to accept, you will find yourself "in" you and not on the outside of you judging what's inside.

As you grow in many of your new techniques for self-awareness, you will begin to see how unique and diverse you are. You are one of the most unusual species in that you each have your own talents and abilities. What is strong in one is often not strong in another. If you are good at one thing you may not be good at another. You may excel in one area and have your limitations in another. You may accept these limitations or you may grow beyond them. You may learn how to be good at everything or you may be happy and satisfied being good at simply "being." It is up to you and your critic. Your critic is in you, and that part of you will not let you rest until you excel. Yet, there is another part of you who is waiting to be born. This part is talent.

Talent is as much a part of you as the nose on your face. You each have a talent. You each have some unique thing that you can do that is as simple and natural for you as breathing. When you find this talent you will be fulfilled. You will begin to move through creation with ease and grace due to its influence. This talent will carry you forward with it. It is your connection to the creative flow. It will give your life meaning and purpose. It is something you love and it brings greater love to you. Liane's talent is channeling books. It has brought her hours and days and even years of tranquil joy. She has moved into a space within herself just by moving words and thoughts through her body. She has ebbed and flowed with this information and she would not stop no matter what. It is a part of her just as breathing is. You too have a talent that is just as much a part of you. Find that talent and you will flow into a new part of you and it will be very good for you.

As you learn to tap into the part of you that brings forth your talent you will be rewarded by you for doing so. This is part of self-service. To serve the self is a very good thing. You are here to serve God. You and God are one. Do not be afraid to be self-serving.

∿

I wish I could share with you how utterly beautiful you are. If I could show you the light that carries you forward you would be dismayed. As you begin to see yourself as greater than simply a body, you will begin to realize that you are in a special place. You are a beam of light that is entering your own creation. You are also the creation that is waiting to be entered. You focus your attention on the creation but that does not take away from the fact that you are also the light. As you grow more and more aware of the light, you will be allowed to do more and more from light. As you evolve and grow in wisdom you automatically become more of your basic essence. Your basic essence is light. Light is the absence of darkness and light is what you are.

Now; as you begin to move on a slide of light, you will be free to take on more light while maintaining what you already have. In the past you have given up light in order to sink deeper into matter. Now you are coming up out of matter and you are evolving spiritually. This is the ability to transform. First you are darkness and disease, then you are light and health. First you are chaos and fear, then you are harmony and love. You have been gradually switching tracks and heading in a new direction.

When you give up your need to be part of matter you will be allowed to rise up out of matter. When you prefer the spiritual to the material you begin to move towards spirit. This is also how you change from darkness to light. You let go of your need to hold on and you begin to flow. This is also how you begin to see your own essence. You begin by acknowledging that you are God creating for God. You then focus on what you have created and you do not judge it. You allow it to be a necessary creation for your particular evolution. You may have desired it one day without realizing how much it would cost you. You may have set it up in order to cost you. Sometimes you do things to get results on another plane. How can you judge from here what you set up from somewhere else? That particular setup may have assisted you in other areas and now you are upset because you do not realize that it did.

Everything you create is to assist you. If you walk out in front of a train you may be experiencing what you need for you. This is all choice! There is no judgment against whatever "choice" you go with. Since this part of you is in the third dimension and has less than a pinpoint of light to guide it, you are in the dark most of the time. When you sit in fear and darkness you begin to see everything through the eyes of fear and darkness. Your vision is distorted by your unawareness and your inability to put more light on any given situation. If you wish to grow beyond ignorance, begin to see through love. Love accepts and allows. Love gives you space to heal. Love gives you patience, and love gives you choices that feel good. If you choose from fear you will stay with fear. If you choose from love you will stay with love.

As you become more and more of love you will be less of fear. Once you are more love, you may decide to choose some of the same things for yourself that you now judge. You may decide that these were good choices after all, and you may decide that more of the same was actually a very good idea. Once you learn how you distort creation you will understand this better.

You are now in a position to switch over to your other viewpoint or perspective. You will find yourself uncertain due to the fact that you can now see both sides in any given situation. You can switch perspectives and you can stay where you are. Once you begin to tune in to everyone else's perspectives as well, you will begin to see everyone from a multi-personality point of view. Everyone has many selves... so do you. As you learn to see how all are being exposed or uncovered at this time, you will begin to realize how no one is simply bad or simply good. Every one of you is everything and when you get right down to it, it is all simply good.

⊰⊱

*A*s you begin to understand the process of evolution to the light, you will gain an awareness and stability. As you move closer and closer to the light, you become un-centered. Your center has always been in darkness and now you are shifting to a center in light. You will know you by knowing your own capabilities and your own frailties. You are not only a frail being at this point in your evolution; you are also a weak light. As you grow stronger, your charge of electrical current will grow and you will emanate a great deal of light. You are one of the greatest forgers and fakes. You imitate what you want and you make yourselves what you are not. You will find that you no longer belong in a false state of being. You are now moving forward into the light and you are growing as you do so. Spiritual awareness is growing and you are becoming all that you must be. You will find that you do not know much about you and how you work. As awareness fills you, you will become acquainted with you. You will begin to see you as you truly are. You will know how you work and you will give you some leeway. This will also allow you to be easier on yourself as you change.

When you become acquainted with yourself, you may discover that you are a child in many respects. There are certain areas of your self who are still maturing and growing. These areas, or parts, may act silly or offensive (in your eyes) and you may want to shut them down. Try not to. Try to teach them as they grow. Talk to them. Talk to yourself and do not be afraid of yourself and your many parts. Be sensitive to them and to their struggle. Be sensitive to the needs of an evolving, growing self. You require nurturing and understanding as you go through this process. You can nurture your "self." You do not require outside assistance. You all know how to give to the self if you will only allow yourself to do so.

As you learn to grow and to nurture and mother your own evolving self you will be healthy and happy. A loved child is a happy child. Love you and care for you like you would a child. Take time with you. Bathe you and touch you with kindness and love. Do not throw yourself roughly into a routine. Do not be pushy and rough with you. Pretend like you are fragile and touch you with kindness. You are usually in such a rush that you do not know how to treat your own body gently. Learn to be gentle with your body. Then you may learn to be gentle with your psyche. You will find that the "self" responds to kindness and gentleness. Are you kind and gentle with you? Do you touch you with love or do you touch you mechanically with precision and habit? Some of you go through your daily routine of shower and shaving and never give a thought to how you treat your "self." Sometime you might want to think about how you might bathe a newborn and the gentleness and kindness you would show towards its psyche and its body. You don't treat fragile things harshly so why would you treat you harshly?

As you continue to grow and learn to nurture your own "self," you will also begin to grow even faster just from the simple act of touching the "self" with love. You may assist you in many ways and you may learn to heal you by loving you. As you do so you will begin to form a bond with your "self." You are your "self" and you deserve to get to know one another. This will also assist you in coming into the self and in coming home to you. You are learning to evolve so that you might return home. Home is where your heart is. Home is where your love is. We are moving into love and we are becoming love. You will love you and you will nurture you, as you are the most precious and the most lovable of life. This is how you evolve and move to the light. Love you and you will grow and expand at such a rate that you will no longer feel the need to receive from outside of yourself. Your own love light will keep you so warm and content that you will no longer run from place to place looking for love, approval and acceptance.

You have the ability and the capability to love you and nurture you and care for you as never before. Take the risk. Give you a little love, and watch you begin to grow and to warm up to you. You will find yourself in a loving relationship with your "self." You will even want to take you out to a good movie and buy yourself flowers for being so wonderful. Learn to love you by starting small. Work your way up and know that there is always more that you can do for you. You will appreciate you for doing this, and that appreciation will grow into more loving acceptance. The more you love and nurture you the more loving and nurturing you become. It is like any profession – if you do not teach how can you still call yourself a teacher? If you do not love how can you be love?

⊰❀⊱

As you learn to be your "self," you will be overwhelmed and dismayed at how wonderful you can feel about you. Your good feelings about you will be grand and over-enthusiastic in character. You will be walking on air and you will feel as though you just fell in love. These feelings will come from you and be about you. You are always feeling good about someone else or something else. For some of you it is your lover and for others it is your child, or pet, or friend. You will begin to feel those good feelings just by knowing you and loving you. In the same way that receiving love and admiration makes you feel good, you will make you feel good. You will know how to love you and how to be a part of you. You will know how to nurture you and make you whole. You will feel complete when you feel loved. You will feel loved when you begin to release the flow of love towards your own self.

As you grow in your own love and admiration, your healing will begin to accelerate. Your love will heal you and allow you to be whole. Your love will make you feel as though you are "special." Special is how you will see your "self" as you grow to know your "self." Most of you never stop to think about your "self" or how you "are" in relation to creation. If you were to be all that you "are," you would take up all of creation. Since you only focus on a pinpoint of you, you take up just a small point in time/space. So, as you learn to focus on more of you, you will see how much space you can actually occupy. You are much more than you believe that you "are." You are much greater than you believe you are. You are God and you think you are unimportant and insignificant and unlovable. When you see how great you are, you will be impressed. You will want to applaud your self just for the simple act of being.

In your day-to-day life I would like you to begin to focus on the things you do that make you feel good about your "self," or about others, or about life. Each day you interact with others, and I want you to begin to *shift* your focus from "every little thing that goes wrong" to "every little thing that goes right." I want you to begin to see how much good is in your life now and how, by focusing on your good, you can create more of the same. Hold the thought of the good you experienced until you no longer see it as small. Hold on to it and fantasize it into something "big!" This is what you do right now with the "little things that go wrong." You fantasize them into greatness. You have this ability to make mountains out of mole hills, and now I want you to use that ability on the "little things that go right." Begin to fantasize them into creations of their own. Start small and get big. If you find a penny begin to imagine finding lots of pennies. Then find quarters and dollars and millions of dollars. In the same way that you allow your mind to roam and to think the worst in any given situation, I now want you to let your mind roam and to think the best.

It will be difficult you know! You're not used to thinking the best and you will want to stop yourself. God forbid you should enjoy your creation of good, but you certainly do enjoy your creation of bad. So; how did you get to this point in time, where you feel free to worry and create fear but you are nervous and refuse to hope for the best? You are afraid of being disappointed. You are afraid of wanting the best. You believe you do not deserve to be "number one" because you were taught to be less than "number one." No one told you that you are the best. No one told you that you are God. They told you not to get too proud or too cocky. Confidence is low in you. You were trained to be respectful of your elders and to care for your loved ones. No one knew to tell you to love you first.

Everyone has been taught how you were taught. Everyone was taught by someone who was taught by someone else. The teaching method has always been the same. "Do not allow them to believe that they are holy. Do not allow them to know that they are God. They may go berserk with power. They may misuse this truth. They may not be ready." I will tell you this now – You are ready to know the truth. If you are reading this material and have not skipped any of it you are ready and your dark side knows what is coming. Your dark side knows that this truth will expose it to the light. The dark portions will act-out if allowed to. You know what to do. You can express your darkness without involving others. You know how to discharge built-up energy, and you know how to defuse you when you are ready to explode. The more you can release in private the less you will create conflict in your relationships.

Now; as you begin to think "big" and dream "big" and make mountains out of little things, I want you to remind yourself that you spend a great deal of time thinking and worrying but, luckily, you only manifest a small amount of what you worry over. In this same way you will only manifest small amounts of what you now dream about. It takes time to get the energies flowing in the direction of bliss when they are so strongly directed towards destruction of bliss.

As you learn to always look for the good and see it and know it, you will gain insight into the strength of this little practice. You will learn to look for the little things every day, and before you know it you will see life as good instead of bad. You will love getting up and being alive. You will love being you and being free of pain and worry. As you heal, you will know more and more freedom from pain and worrying until, eventually, pain and worry will fall away never to be seen or heard from again. You will then have a pain-free, worry-free existence and you will be loving you and your existence. Most of you do not love the idea of existing. We will change that for you. You are on your way now and you have done well. Now get out there and find lots of good reasons to exist and to love you!

≈⟋≈

You will come to know how you operate by watching and seeing how you create for yourself. You are the one who is in charge of your life even though you do not believe that you are. You are the one who is connected to creation and you are the one who is God the Creator. After you learn to accept that you are God you will be allowed to see how you create as God. Most of you are in a position to see how you create little things in your life, but you have not yet accepted that you create big things as well. When you finally see yourself as God and with your own nature of creative force, you will be seeing yourself as the one who makes all things occur in your created world. For now I will talk to you from where you are and this will allow you to relate to what I have to say.

When you learn to release your hold on who you are and allow yourself to become something or someone new, you will begin to grow into an entirely new you. You will move out of the need to control your destiny and you will flow with destiny. Destiny has its way of working with you and despite you if it must. The only thing that destiny does not do is push you out into it. You move into future destinations by pushing yourself out in them. You create your future out of your present and mixed with your past. If you fear your past or any part of it, it will color your future with fear. If you clean out your past it will assist you in having a clear, bright future. Everything that happens is for you and by you. There are no accidents and there are no parts you did not play that you should have played. You are right where you are meant to be. You are here to grow, and growth takes time and growth takes learning.

You are learning and growing as a school room experiment would. You are the seed and you are the one who planted the seed. You grow and look for the one who created you and that one is you. You are inside you and outside you. You are here and you are everywhere else. You are in a state of unconsciousness and you are becoming conscious. You are evolving and growing and you are watching as you evolve and grow. The Creator and the created are one. You are hurt because the part of you who is growing does not know about the part of you who is watching over it so lovingly. You left part of you to be separate and to research life. Now part of you is afraid and alone, but that part is just a tiny fraction and the rest of you is coming "in" to say, "I am with you, you are no longer alone. I am God and I created you and I love you. You are a part of me and you are being watched over. Do not fear death, do not fear change. I am watching and loving you. You are not alone. You are me and I love all of me."

As you learn to recognize more of your created evolution for what it is, you will begin to let go of judgment and blame. You will begin to see how you are on a path and it has had a few stumbling blocks here and there, but you can learn to see them differently and, by doing so, change what they are. As you learn to see things through the eyes of acceptance and to allow events to occur, you will create trust and a flow to your life. You are still very much afraid of not being accepted and this is due to the fact that *you have a problem with acceptance!*

~~~

As you learn to be free of the ropes that have restricted you and bound you, you will find yourself in new and uncharted territory. You will find yourself walking in directions you have never before walked in. As you learn to allow for freedom of choice, your choices begin to expand. This expansion will allow you to see the greater variety of opportunities that surround you. You are moving into more of you and you are thus expanding and stretching you. This creates a set up whereby you may begin to see a great deal more than your limited perspective has ever brought you. As you see how you create situations by your attitude and your nuance to any given situation, you will begin to understand why and how things in your life work out the way that they do. You will begin to understand how your attitude affects not only your life but the lives of others and their response to you and your attitude.

You get back what you give out and most of you do not have a clue as to the subtle messages you are sending out. You are afraid and defensive and you protect your fear and your defenses in many ways. You then sit and wonder why so and so reacted this way to you. You also wonder why you can't have a smooth flowing life with no struggle. It is your inner workings and your projected energy. You are toxic and you hurt and you are getting back at yourself, or God, or the world for your pain. You believe so strongly in an "eye for an eye," or "blind justice," that you are continuing a cycle that began as far back as Adam and Eve. Justice is not punishment and justice is not getting back at yourself and life. Justice is freedom and justice is being rewarded not enslaved.

As you learn to set yourself free you will also learn that you need not try to fix everyone (including yourself). Everyone is being fixed and everything is in order. You are confused and you too are being fixed. God is the part of everything that is intelligence and wisdom. God is light. The light is coming in and taking over. There is no missing it. It is here. You cannot avoid it. It is part of you. It is in you. It is growing in you. It is in your neighbor and it is in everything you see. Once you begin to feel this light presence in your life you will be feeling trust. You will feel like everything is good and right in your life. This will be trust and faith. You will trust what is here and you will trust where you are going. Trust is very powerful and I love trust. It feels so good!

Now; often I have told you to invite God in, that God does not enter uninvited. Well, that was only to get you to focus on asking. God is expedited in this way. The light is rushed in as the doors are open and receptive. There are many things that I will tell you to get you to receive. If I tell you that you have a twin soul who is looking for you, you will begin to open to the idea that you are lovable and that love is looking for you. As you open to this idea you begin a shift within you that allows you to be loved. You literally create it by your attitude and your belief. When you hold in mind that you have a twin soul who will make you happy you begin to create the reality that someone is there just for you. This is true. Someone is there just for you, and you will draw that someone when you have cleared you and turned on your light.

So; as we go through this process of stretching and growing I will show you how to look, or project your focus, in this direction or that direction. What this does is put light on the direction you are led to focus on. If you have fear and darkness in that direction (or that corner of you), you will then begin to heal by the simple fact that you have focused "light" or "awareness" in that direction. Once the "shift" or healing begins, you will know it because the unhealed stuff will come to the surface and you will walk around saying, "Oh no, how much more can I take," or, "Oh no, I thought I had already healed that." You heal in cycles as you are taking off the layers of you. You are round like an onion with layers. You have dark spots on you and each layer that is peeled may contain part of the dark spot from the layer before it. You have as many dark spots as you do wounds. If you are very wounded you will continue to heal until all the dark spots are gone. They seem to get smaller and less charged with pain as you reach the smaller layers of you (the onion you).

You are in a process of healing that may take some time but it does end. This healing does not go on forever. You begin to regain strength and your spirit is set free to guide you and to nurture you. This is a process of releasing you from your prison and allowing you to be free of pain, judgment, illness, stress, struggle, envy, jealousy and any number of restricted emotions. You are going to operate from love and light. Love and light are here for you and you will be well rewarded for your efforts in freeing you of fear.

This entire process is about leaving fear behind. Can you imagine a life without fear? Can you imagine a pain-free existence? Can you imagine a life without struggle? No – you cannot, and the reason you cannot is because you have never known such a life. It is time. It can be achieved and it is being created by you. By the simple fact that you are clearing fear from your body, you are changing your programming. Your programming says to fear everything. Your new found wisdom and enlightenment says that you have nothing to fear and that you were lied to. You will find that your new programming will take over and gain momentum and begin to create for you. This does not occur overnight. Not yet anyway. You have not developed your creative skills to that level just yet. So; your biggest challenge in this process is patience. Can you be patient enough with yourself to allow yourself to go through the healing or peeling process? Can you?

⚶

As you continue to stretch and to grow you will begin to feel as though you can conquer your world. You will also begin to see how you create your world. Your world is how you view it and your world does not have to be difficult. Did you ever notice how, sometimes, when you are not feeling well, even the simplest task seems difficult? It is because you are weak and confused, and you know that when you regain your energy you will easily complete your task. This is how you are evolving now. You are clearing in order to heal. You are being peeled and layered and you are weak. When you are weak you have a hard time thinking straight and coping with situations.

Once you regain your strength and energy you will feel great and life will feel great. Your fears are going and, as they surface, they begin to send signals. These signals confuse you and you feel like you are afraid and falling apart. Well, in a sense you are. But in another sense you are simply feeling what is moving up and out of you. How can you not feel fear as it moves from its hiding place within you? It moves through you in order to leave. You will feel it as it goes. You may even react or overreact to it. Do not. Try to stay calm and remind yourself that when fear is gone you will be fearless and you will love life.

As you continue to love and to grow, you will find yourself wanting to be loved and wanting to grow even more. This whole process is only painful in the beginning. It is like the surgery that removes the unwanted poison from your body. It hurts while you are feeling it, but once you heal, you actually feel better and soon you forget the soreness and pain from the initial surgery.

You will find that once you begin your healing process, you will know more confidently that you are on your way to Nirvana. You will begin to flow with the healing process and to trust that God is on your side and not against you. God is so much on your side that he/she is you... in you, on you, around you, in the air that you breathe. God never leaves you but you may ignore God and refuse to take God in. This is how you shut out light. Ignorance has created a big shift downward on the spiral of light. Intelligence will shift you upward and, as you go upward, the spiral not only gains momentum it also expands and the circles are bigger. This is how you are growing and being stretched. You are going up the spiral instead of down it. You are becoming bigger spiritually and smaller physically. I know that this makes no sense to you now, but you will grasp it in time.

You are learning to be all that you can, and you must be patient in order to allow yourself to develop properly. You need not rush or push at yourself to change. Feed you the correct information and all parts of you will begin to respond. When you receive new input you begin to shift to a new perspective or direction. When you receive lots of new input you begin to shift very quickly.

As you know, you are being guided and watched and looked after. One of the reasons you believe you are alone is that you have boundaries that keep you limited. You crave human acceptance because your boundaries block the acceptance you would otherwise receive from within. We are going to shift your boundaries and this may rock your foundation. You may change drastically as my pen has or you may keep it more subtle and a slower process. You still may make a drastic change or shift. It may be acceptable to those around you or it may be rejected by those around you. After all, like attracts like and if you change what you are, you are no longer like what you were. If your friends change too... great. If not, you will draw 'like' to you. And when you change again you may shift and lose a few and gain a few.

This is why I tell you to let go. New is coming – old is leaving. You are becoming new and leaving the old behind. A lot of times you are drawn together by your pain. One wounded animal draws or attracts another. You will lick one another's wounds until you heal and feel better. That is the point where you begin to draw those who are also healing. Then, when you have healed, you will draw those who have healed. And when you are in Nirvana you will be with others who are in a state of ascended bliss. It is natural to attract to you what you are and to change who you draw by changing who you are or where you are.

As you experience these shifts and changes please remember that your mirrors are only what you want them to be. You create them to show yourself who and what you are. As you grow and achieve acceptance within your own self, you will draw those who accept you and appreciate you. You will surround yourself with those who love you once you have achieved the gift of self love. You are on your way now. The first step to self love is clearing out the fear that has divided you and kept you away from love. You are love and you are light. We are connecting you to that part of you just by making you aware that it exists in you.

☙❧

*A*s you grow in spiritual awareness you will find that you no longer believe you are bad. With this belief comes your salvation. Once you reconsider and determine that you are innocent, you will drop the need for self punishment. As you move into a place of non-punishment you will begin to allow yourself to come out of suffering. Suffering is feeding off of a "need to punish in order to release guilt." Once you let go of this need to punish in order to release guilt you will feel better. Right now you are so programmed to punish because you believe that it is the only thing that works. Once you let go of this need, you will be ending the tyrant role you have played with yourself. You will come out of shame and guilt because you will no longer have you ruling over you and shouting how awful you are. The funny (or maybe sad) part is that you actually do not know that you constantly criticize yourself every day. Your voice is so constant and so accustomed to free reign that it controls you and it does not receive interference from you.

You have a voice that tells you on a daily basis how unattractive you are and how unworthy you are. This voice was programmed into you years ago and now it rules your behavior towards yourself and others. This voice is also the voice who selects how your day will go and how you will behave towards others. This voice says, "You are right, don't let them tell you how to do things." This voice also says, "You are better than what they think." When, in actuality the voice is the one who is thinking poorly of you and putting you down. But the voice must have somewhere to place the blame and the blame goes wherever the voice directs it. So you all walk around blaming everyone and everything instead of catching the voice and saying, "Shut up! You have tricked me and deceived me long enough." Listen today. Listen for that voice that is so critical and demanding. It will begin softly and nag and nag until you explode with nervous energy, or with anger at someone else. Catch your voice and tell it to wise up, that things are changing and you are no longer going to criticize who you are. As a matter of fact you are no longer going to criticize anyone or anything. Begin to teach your voice to listen and to learn a new way.

As you learn to observe your inner workings, you will begin to see how you self-sabotage the good things that come your way. Some of you have even gotten very creative about making a good thing look like a bad thing. Some of you even see everything as awful so you will never have to receive your good. Too much good and you will feel guilty and you cannot handle any more guilt. You are so afraid of feeling guilty because you judge yourself as guilty, and then you set out to find various ways to punish yourself for being bad. This is all done with the assistance of the voice of your critical self and the part of you who believes in an eye for an eye. So now we have you talking bad about you in your own head. No wonder you go crazy when someone else talks bad about you or puts you down. Your head is already so full of your own putdowns that you can't handle that coming from others. Your cup is full and running over with putdowns.

Now; as you grow in spiritual awareness you will become aware of these parts of you. You will also become aware of the part of you who is out for revenge. This part will be big in those who have repressed such thoughts and feelings. He/she/you will act and feel better than others. It is like you are smarter and you feel good by the fact that others are stumbling and not doing so well. This is righteous behavior and some of you may become quite self-righteous as you come into balance. You see, in order to heal the unbalanced parts, you must go into them and acknowledge them. In this way, you begin to contact and bring into balance all parts of you. As you do so, your critic in your head (the voice) may grow and get out of control, and your perception of how awful you are may grow until you begin to balance.

You all react differently when you believe you are awful. Some will hide in their shame, others will throw their shame out at someone else hoping to get rid of it, and others will just feel awful and get sick. It is different for everyone. You will clear this area as judgment leaves and you will then be free to look for the good in everything. Do not be afraid. It is only you learning to love you and to release what has always been a part of you. You no longer require or need judgment and so criticism must go. There is no need to criticize, judge and punish. You are breaking the karmic cycle. No more "redoing" to get out the guilt. Now you simply let go of guilt by not blaming anyone.

Let go of punishment as you do so, for punishment is no longer necessary if there was no wrong done. The prisoner will be set free and you will no longer be frozen in a state of unbalance and pain. You will come into balance and pain will leave. You will be free of evil which is energy that is blocked in your body and running your life. You will begin to run on light and no longer required dark energy to control you. Dark is dense. Light is light. You will find that you are moving into the spirit of life and away from the draining energy of illness and "disease." Your life will move into "ease" and you will flow with all life.

෴

*A*s you learn to accept you and to enjoy you, you will find that you are quite nice and you are even beautiful. Most of you do not know what true beauty is and you are confused and think it is looking like a model. To look like a model is fashionable, but what is "fashionable" changes with taste. Taste has to do with likes and dislikes, and so you end up with a body and a face that you either like or dislike.

So; who taught you to judge your body and face as desirable to look upon? Your parents had a great deal to do with it. If you had parents who were in balance and self-loving, maybe you see your face and body as beautiful. If you had parents who were out of balance and unloving towards the self, you may have a tough time learning to appreciate your beauty. You do not need to hear that you are ugly to believe that you are. You may have picked up from your parents that it is bad to like your looks. It is vain in some belief systems and it is not acceptable. So, as you grew you began to try harder to look presentable and, in some cases, you may have simply given up and let yourself go. If it's not desirable or good to find beauty in yourself why try? Well, this type of thinking is what is making you believe you are unworthy. When you believe that you are unworthy, you begin to take things away from you and to punish you. When you begin to believe that you are worthy, you will give things back to you and you will see the beauty in you.

When you discover true beauty you will love yourself even more. You will begin to open up to joy... the joy of self... the joy of being you... the joy of living in you. As you learn to love and accept yourself, you will learn to see your own goodness and kindness and your struggles will end. You will begin to treat you with love and understanding, and you will begin to know that you are no longer a villain. You have been your own worst critic and worst enemy since you were first taught how bad you can be. You have always wanted to love you but did not know how to. You have always known you were good, but you were programmed to believe otherwise. You are an "angel of God." How can you not be beautiful? How can you be bad if you are a spirit of God? Much has to change within you in order for you to realize this truth. Much has to go in order for you to come into the light and out of the darkness.

You are an angel of God! Think about that all day today and you will find you treating yourself with respect. Respect and honor must be given to you... to your body. Do you respect your body or do you simply push it and shove it around. Maybe, if you are smart, you will see a big reflection here. If you run your body until it is exhausted and drops, you may see how others expect you to run until you are exhausted and drop. There is a healthy respect for material gain on your planet and very little respect for you... your body... the house that you live in. You poison it without a second thought. You fill it with chemicals and smoke and you have poor eating and maintenance habits. How do you expect it to serve you undyingly? You must begin to respect and love the house that you live in. It is you! You are part of it. Stop worrying about your neighbor and how he/she is polluting the environment. Stop worrying about the poor children and their future. Look at you! Look at the house you live in and how little respect and honor you show it. It is you!

As you grow and learn to develop your intuitive abilities, you will find that you do not require fear or logic to be insightful. You will begin to see a significant improvement in the way you deal with life and with all situations which occur during one's life. As you grow in perspective, you also see how you might learn to adapt more easily to the flow of change. Change has been difficult for you from the beginning, and it is not always what you want. As you see yourself adapting and changing in new directions, you will begin to feel good about this process. You will find your strength by looking at your weakness. You will see where you are strong by seeing where you are weak. You may travel this line of energy and begin to change your weak areas into strong ones.

As you develop, you will begin to achieve a greater sense of self. This will enable you to come out of denial and face yourself with all your truths and lies. You will be exposing you to you. You will be seeing for the first time how you jeopardize your own "self." You will begin to see how you block and destroy your own good. You wanted to destroy bad, and good is the same as bad. Good runs the same line of energy. If you draw a circle and draw a line through the middle, you will see the line as whole. If you put bad at one end of this line and good at the opposite end, you now have polarities. Do not polarize! Do not separate and divide your lines of energy. Allow everything to simply "be."

You will find that as you change and grow and expand and stretch, you will become bigger, brighter and more receptive. The bigger you are the more you can hold. So; do not judge situations which create expansion and growth and stretching in you. You may say, "Oh no! Here we go again," but do not block and push away. Try to flow. Try to "allow" everything to be okay. Try to be "open" and go with what is occurring... "You lost your job, oh no, how dreadful...!" or... "You lost your job, wow, what a wonderful opportunity for growth and change! Let's see where this will lead you." Look for the good in everything. Good and bad are just what *you decide* to call this particular line of energy. Sometimes you choose bad, sometimes you choose good. Know good. Begin to look for good. Allow good to be seen and felt and received. You have looked for and found bad for long enough.

Gain insight into energy by knowing that you change all energy into what you believe it should be. You are programmed to "watch out for" and "look out for" and "be careful of" evil. "Evil will sneak up on you and get you!" "Evil is bad and you will burn in hell fire and damnation for being evil." You fear evil and you look for it at every turn. If you do not understand something... such as hatred, you call it evil. You are ignorant to the extent that you are all superstitious. Fear of the unknown is so pronounced in you that you literally fear your own selves because you are unknown to you.

You create things and situations and you do not know it is you, so then you judge what you have created as awful or bad. Give evil and bad a rest. Let it go! Switch over to good and pleasure! Most of you are so confused that you believe pleasure to be bad... "Don't get too high off life or you're out-of-control with bliss! Don't get too comfortable or happy or you'll be let down and hurt." These beliefs are very strong in you and you are very good at finding the bad or "what's wrong" instead of finding the good or "what's right." Do not be afraid to "receive." When you receive, you actually begin to open up. Do not be afraid to open up. You will not get hurt. You may grow and you may stretch and you may even change. Do not be afraid of change. Look for the good in change! Do not look for the bad.

You are criticizing your "self" and your world to death. You are killing and narrowing your world to death. It is disintegrating right beneath you. You are killing it by your negative perceptions and your limited belief in reality. "Give love a chance." Open to love and allow love to rule the day. God is love. Would God lead you astray? No, I think not. God is love. How can love have ulterior motives? Love is joy, peace, happiness, caring, sharing, playing, enjoying life. Learn to enjoy life. Learn to love. You may find love by finding good and letting go of bad. You do not require instant gratification. What you do require is trust that you are good, and God is good and life is good. Stop changing these energies into something else. Look at your "perceptions" and how you "use" them. It's all you doing this to you!

≈≀≋

As you learn to know your own inner workings you will begin to see how you create your outer reality. The inner reality is projected outward on the screen of your life. You then begin to relate to what you see. This is, in essence, relating to what is inside of you. Your relationship to your self is what you call "life." Sometimes you like what you get and sometimes you do not.

As you learn to recognize what you create and accept it as a good thing, you will begin to feel comfortable creating your life. You will begin to see how and even why you created certain situations. You will even begin to know what you are creating before you create it. You will become proficient at being your own creator. You will learn to love your inner projections and to relate well with them as they appear on your outer screen. You will even find that your relating, or relationship with you, will improve dramatically. You will no longer see you as an enemy who projects rotten situations for you to deal with. You will begin to recognize that there is a plan and a purpose for you and for your life pattern. As you see this plan, you will become more comfortable with the "idea" that you are your own creation as well as the instrument by which you were created. You are God and God is all things, so that makes you all things. You are the one who decides which, out of all things, will be created for you on any specific day!

You are the one who is doing everything in your life. You are the actor and producer and the screen upon which you view life. You are life and you are the cause of your life. You did not accidentally drop out of the sky and land in your mother's womb. You consciously created a situation whereby you could be born and then you projected into that situation. Voilà! We now have a baby growing and taking on life. You literally create what will occur and how and when. You make you late for delivery or you make you early. You also ask a friend to join you and we will see twins, or more, if you so desire. This is how powerful you are. You go in knowing and you come out deaf and dumb to any conscious choice you made. You are now being born and it hurts. You do not remember coming into the womb or why. You only know that you are being pushed out and it is uncomfortable and, of course, since you don't remember why you are here, it is confusing.

So; as we go along we will try to alleviate some of your concern and confusion. You do not know who you are or why you are here, and this is what causes stress for you. You create things that you do not realize you do, and you react in ways that create other things that frighten you even more. Cause and effect is well known, and cause and effect is what you are. You are the cause and you are the effect.

Now; as you learn to recognize when you are causing something to occur, you may begin to see how you create. By becoming *aware* of your own actions and reactions you may stop self-sabotage which is very big in all of you. This, of course, is due to your own need for punishment, which came as a direct result of your belief in "an eye for an eye." You believe that you cannot be forgiven without sacrifice or repentance. Now you are seeing the results of your belief. Change your belief and you change cause and effect. You may change any cause and effect from inside of you. You create from inside and project outward.

So; those of you who insist on changing the world you see are really wasting your energy. Work on the inside and you will see greater results. You will be creating a stronger image to project outward, and this will create a big shift in your causal world. Your inner world is full of holes. You are healing these holes and wounds by accepting responsibility for you and your creations. Be whole by allowing you to know you. Spend time with you. Talk with you! Talk to your voices. Who are they? What do they want from you? Why do they criticize and nag you? How can you integrate this part of you if you believe that to talk with your various parts is sick or crazy? You have been taught to believe that you must act and react in a certain fashion or you will be an outcast to society. Do not listen. These are old, ignorant, superstitious beliefs. The new belief is "relate to the self." Know thy self. To know you is to love you!

$\mathcal{A}$s you learn to see your patterns and habits you will begin to see how you have been programmed. You will also begin to see where you may wish to change your programming and how you might take on a whole new perspective in any given situation. Once you learn to recognize how you are the one who took on certain beliefs, you will be allowed to release those same beliefs. You are no longer going to be a victim of your own creative force. You are going to learn to stay centered and to know that you are creating from within you. You are going to realize that you are the one who is in you and you are the one who is creating for you. You have no one to blame but you. Stop blaming you, and begin to work with you and to allow you to be what you were meant to be.

You are in a position now to become very independent and to learn responsibility of the self. This is a big step for you, and it also will allow you to see more clearly how you are not only your own "cause," you are also your own "effect." As you learn to recognize the parts of you that cause certain aspects to occur in your life, you might begin to know you better and to recognize how versatile you are. You are in a position to be even greater than you realize and to show even greater acceptance of who you are. At some point you will consciously begin to see how you create it all and how you are living in it as you create it. You created a world and then you projected into it to see how it would fit. From time to time you might want to change how you view it in order to change how it fits you or suits you.

You may begin to discover that you want to start over and allow everything to be new. This too is possible. Everything and anything is possible. It is only necessary to see where you are and you will be connecting to you. You are only in this process because you created it. You created it because you wanted to experience creation. You now have creation, and you now have the ability to receive (on a conscious level) everything that you have (up until now) created on an unconscious level. Unconsciousness is growing into consciousness. The dark is being dissipated by the light. The light is taking over. Awareness is coming in and it is being accepted by you. As you receive greater amounts of light you will feel "stretched" in a new direction. It is how you are changing direction. You once went down, now you are switching and going "up." This is ascension. You are rising up out of ignorance and unconscious behavior.

As you learn to go deeper and deeper into your own psyche, you will be activating parts of you and you will be allowing parts of you to become what they were meant to become. So much of you has been suppressed and repressed out of a "need to hide things." This "need to hide things" comes from a clear belief that you are guilty of something. You know, Jesus did not die on a cross for you so you would not have to. He did it so you would recognize how you have no sins. You are all sinners in that you all make mistakes and sometimes you make unconscious and ignorant choices. But, as you know, God does not condemn.

So; who has done all this judging and condemning that goes on? Maybe, just maybe, it is fear and ignorance. Maybe, just maybe, it is a part of you who is uncomfortable with the belief that "everything is God no matter what it is." Maybe, just maybe, you are stuck in judgment and ignorant behavior. Maybe, just maybe, you are about to "forgive you" and set yourself and all mankind free!

As you learn to grow beyond your current restrictions and limitations, you will begin to see how you can expand your belief system and actually create more good for yourself. The only reason you do not see the good now is that you are stuck in the belief that life is bad and dangerous. If, when you were born, you were taught that everything is good and everything serves a purpose, you would not get so upset by everything that occurs. But when you are taught to "watch out or they will hurt you," you begin to look for the danger and hurt. Now you have found danger and hurt. Now I encourage you to look for sunshine and happiness. I want you to believe with your heart that you are creating good for yourself. I want you to know that your gifts are many and you will receive abundance and joy.

You are on a path to bliss. You are clearing away the old beliefs and creating new ones. You are coming alive with new energy and awareness. You are being born new and you are going to begin to create from that newness. Let go of the past and let go of the old belief system that warns you to "beware" and "be wary of." You are now learning to trust and to grow in trust. You are learning to trust you and to know you as your creator. You are learning to allow for mistakes because you know that mistakes are simply growth, which is how you get where you are going. Mistakes allow you to learn and to be aware next time. How can a mistake be bad? Actually, how can a mistake even be considered a mistake?

You are now at a turning point as a civilization. You are taking on greater amounts of light and you are shedding darkness. This may cause you to feel as though you are being stripped, and basically, you are. You are shedding parts of you that no longer serve you. When you were going "down" to grow your roots it was a necessary part of you. Now you are going "up" to begin to bloom. This part of your natural evolution requires you to be free of the restrictions that were necessary in the downward thrust. You are moving faster now and so you may find that you are creating more quickly. You are learning and growing and stretching. Mistakes assist you in your growth. Be thankful for your mistakes. They are a big gift. You have been confused for a very long time now, and you find it necessary to judge and condemn yourself and others for mistakes. No one really makes mistakes. Everyone is simply learning and evolving and this is how it is done.

So; give yourself a break and forgive yourself for all those mistakes you "thought" you made. You were mistaken about mistakes. Be careful how you judge the gifts of life. You may turn anything positive and good into a negative bad thing. You have the ability to do this because you are "creator."

❧

As you learn how to recognize those parts of you who are punishing you, you will begin to know how you "feel like a victim." Even though you may consciously feel like a tough guy or gal, the part of you who is being bullied feels like a victim. This part of you is very much like your own private judge and jury. This part of you is also very much like your own hangman. Once you learn to forgive yourself for everything you have ever done, your hangman will be out of work. He will need to be retrained for a new job. Once this is accomplished you will find him very good at giving you gifts. This, of course, is the opposite of taking away gifts.

Once you come into balance you will be allowed to receive and to know that you are "deserving." Once you find this area of your life you will be quite happy with yourself. Once you are happy with yourself you will let go of your belief that you are no good. You will turn self-loathing and low self-esteem into a thing of the past. Once you learn to see how you have made a mistake in judgment regarding your own nature, you will be able to let it be.

Your nature will be free of rules and restrictions, and you will rise to a level of love and understanding that will allow you to flow with all of nature.

You are now in a process of letting go of your need to block the natural flow of life. You are now in a process that will allow you to see how you have created things to look one way when, in actuality, they are another. You will find that, as you allow more of you to express, you will be accepting more of nature or your natural self. Do not be afraid of parts of you that you do not understand. At this point in your evolution you are so limited in your understanding that you do not grasp even the smallest of concepts. You are growing and learning but you are still so immature in thought and belief. This is what is changing and this is what will create a bright future for you.

You have the ability to change anything and to create anything. It helps if all parts of you are focused on this concept and that they all go in the same direction. When you have major beliefs that disrupt what is going on you will destroy what is going on. You must get you to move into wholeness, by allowing all parts of you to emerge. You are afraid to allow all parts to emerge because you are afraid to hear voices telling you things that you do not wish to hear. You are also afraid of these voices even if they never speak to you. You all fear the voice in your head. You actually have many, but you are afraid to acknowledge it because you have been taught to fear hearing voices. Only schizophrenics and crazy people hear voices, and you do not want to be one of those so you shut yourself down and you never get to know you. You are missing out on an opportunity to integrate and know your own self by being afraid of part of you.

The part of you that can speak to you is not dangerous. It is simply out of touch with you. You live in you, and yet you hold yourself apart from parts of you out of fear. *You fear you!* You fear who you are and what you are and what you do not understand. *You have no grasp or understanding of you.* You have been taught to be afraid of certain aspects of your own self. Why do you think that you wither and die? You are afraid of your own self. You frighten you by your very existence. You are the only being who does not like themselves. You are the only creation who is taught to not trust or communicate with the self. You are taught to stay away from the self and yet you are the self. This is separation. It is you killing you by fragmentation to the extreme. *You will continue to die until you are taught how to live.* No one ever taught you how to live with you and how to get along with you.

You now have the opportunity to go into a relationship with you by allowing all parts of you to express themselves to you; not to a doctor, not to a psychiatrist, but to you. You are going to learn who you are and what you think and what you believe. This is done through self communication. Talk to yourself and listen to yourself and do not judge or be afraid of what comes out. You are learning that "you" are "in" you, and the only one to fear is "you." Stop fearing you. Get to know you and then you will know how to "accept" you. You will love you once you can "accept" you.

꧁

As you begin to see how you are only what you were taught, you will begin to re-teach yourself. You will grow and you will learn. You will begin to know through developing your own intuitional and receptive abilities. You will learn to use all parts of you for your own growth and development. As you learn to accept certain parts of you, you actually assist them in changing and growing. Just by "realizing" that you have a dysfunctional part, you begin to re-create it into something more functional. If you have a flat tire and you will not admit to yourself that you do, you will eventually be driving on a rim and destroy it. This will cause you to pull over and ask "what's wrong." Don't be surprised when you are told that you should have paid attention when you were driving and you would have "felt" the flat tire. If you think things are out of whack with your driving it is coming from you. You need to look at how you perform and admit that you are not very bright! You will be soon, but, for now, you must find the parts that are working against you and allow them to work for you.

As you learn to target your own dysfunctional areas you will begin to bring them into the spotlight. By looking at them you actually move them into awareness which is light. You shed light on them, and then they can be cleaned out and transformed into something more functional and performance-perfect for your new life as the new you.

Gradually you will get in touch with parts of you that you may like or you may not like. They have all served you for a long time and they may not give up without a fight. You will feel exhausted and drained when these parts begin to slug it out inside of you. You will be fighting and struggling with parts of you until they "give up and come into awareness." Awareness is the light, and it is well known that when you bring a stupid or superstitious belief to the surface of consciousness it must evaporate. Ignorance cannot maintain its power in the light of awareness. Darkness must dissolve when the light goes on. You will be left with light! These parts do not freely wish to come forward, so you must find them and bring them forward.

So; how do you find them? You might try having a conversation with yourself and find out what you really think and feel. You might try communicating with you. You spend all day and all night and your whole life with you. Don't you think it's a little bit odd that you have been "trained" to believe that it's not good to talk with yourself? Think about it. Really, really "think" about it. If you were to come into the world on your own and there was no one else here, would you talk to and listen to you, or would you continue to ignore you for the rest of your days on earth within you? Would you simply live and die without communicating or asking any questions of yourself? Would you simply spend all your time thinking and no time communicating?

You are going to learn that you are not at all what you were taught you are. You are not here simply to eat, drink and be merry. You have a purpose and you have a plan. If you can begin to see that you are part of the big plan, you will begin to open that doorway to awareness. The more awareness you can bring in, the greater the light becomes. Just think! You bring in light. You dispel darkness. You are creating the light where it was once dark. You are the Creator. God is light. You are the light and you are bringing you forward. You are receiving you, and you are the part that is being received. You are the light, and you are the sender and the receiver of light. You play a very big role in creation "if you choose to."

You are the light of the world. The light will lift "you." You are lifting you up and you are being lifted up. You are very, very powerful and you think you are only what you see. You see so little and there is so much more. I will teach you to see more. I will show you a new way to see you. When you see you in a new "light," you will dissolve the old darkness that fills you. You will become light by shifting awareness. This is a gradual process. You are so layered with gunk and sludge that it takes time to un-layer you and dissolve the muck and mire that has clogged you. You will do well to clean you out on a daily basis and this will assist you in bringing in light.

You have completed a great deal of information so far in this series of books. Stay tuned for our next en"lighten"ing book titled *Love Conquers All*. You will enjoy it I am certain. Until then I will say "farewell" and a fond "thank you" to Liane for not quitting when she feels like it.

God's Pen

I first heard the voice of God in 1988. I was sitting in my back yard reading a book when this big booming voice interrupted with, "I am God and I will not come to you by any other name." I felt like the voice was everywhere – inside of me as well as in the sky around me. I was so frightened that I ran in my bedroom to hide.

This was not the first time that I heard voices. I had been communicating with my own spirit guide or soul for about a year. I guess my depth of fear regarding God, and all that he represented to me at the time, was just too much.

I spent two days trying to avoid the voice of God, which was patiently waiting for me to respond. By the second day I was exhausted from lack of sleep and decided to give in and talk with him. This turned out to be the greatest gift and best decision of my life.

The first book, *God Spoke through Me to Tell You to Speak to Him*, shows my evolution from communicating with my soul to communicating with the Big Guy. It took a couple years for me to be comfortable communicating with God. My fear of a punishing God was big! That has most definitely changed and I now think of God as my partner and best friend.

In the beginning the voice of God would wake me in the middle of the night and tell me it was time to write. He said I had promised to do this work (I assumed he was talking about the soul/spirit me). I would drag myself up to a sitting position and watch in amazement as my hand flew across the page, while I tried to keep up by reading what was being written.

It was always so much fun to wake up the next morning and grab my notebook to see what God had written during the night. After some time the voice stopped waking me and I became comfortable picking up my pen and writing for God first thing in the morning. I think in the beginning I had to be awakened while still semi-conscious from sleep so I wouldn't object too much to the information that was being channeled through me.

As I grew less and less afraid (and more trusting) of God, he was able to communicate greater information. Some of the information is quit controversial, but I felt it important to just let it be and not censor it. I present the writings here to you as they were given to me. I have edited a little (mostly the more personal information regarding myself) and I have used a pen name for privacy reasons. I asked God for a good pen name and he guided me to Liane which (I was told) in Hebrew means "God has answered."

At one point I became a little concerned about my sanity in all this, so I went to a hypnotherapist to find out what I was doing. Under hypnosis I saw this incredibly huge beam of light with a voice coming from within it. It was a giant "loving light" and felt so comforting and kind. It felt like that's where I came from. After that I stopped worrying about my sanity. If this is crazy, I think it's a very good kind of crazy to be....

In loving light, Liane

Loving Light Books

Available at:
Loving Light Books: www.lovinglightbooks.com
Amazon: www.amazon.com
Barnes & Noble: www.barnesandnoble.com

Also Available on Request at Local Bookstores

www.ingramcontent.com/pod-product-compliance
Lightning Source LLC
LaVergne TN
LVHW011241080426
835509LV00005B/586